history at source

IMPERIAL AND WEIMAR GERMANY

1890-1933

John Laver

2

Hodder & Stoughton

LONDON SYDNEY AUCKLAND

The cover illustration is a detail from *Pillars of Society*, painted by George Grosz 1926, courtesy The National Gallery, Berlin.

British Library Cataloguing in Publication Data
Laver, John
   Imperial and Weimar Germany, 1890-1933. —
(History at Source Series)
   I. Title   II. Series
   943.08

ISBN 0–340–57167–5

First published 1992

Typeset by Litho Link Ltd, Welshpool, Powys, Wales
Printed in Great Britain for the educational publishing division of Hodder & Stoughton Ltd, Mill Road, Dunton Green, Sevenoaks, Kent by Page Bros. Ltd, Norwich

CONTENTS

PREFACE

Modern German history has long been a popular topic with students studying at A level, AS level, Higher Grade and beyond. Changes in the requirements of examination boards, particularly the introduction of source-based questions, coursework and personal assignments, have not decreased the popularity of the topic, but have increased the demands on students and teachers alike.

This book is intended for students, and hopefully teachers, who are interested in a number of key topics in modern German history and would benefit from a practical complement to existing textbooks and monographs. Too often the history of modern Germany has been treated as merely a prelude to Nazi Germany rather than a topic worthy of study in its own right. Certainly the history of the post-1933 period cannot be understood without an appreciation of the Weimar Republic, but the latter should be regarded as more than a prelude to the main performance. Some understanding of pre-First World War Germany is also essential to an appreciation of the issues which concerned Germans after 1918. The issue of continuity is one which is raised in this collection of sources. A study of Bismarck's Germany would also be relevant, but beyond the scope of the present book; but I make no apologies for treating the period 1890-1933 both as a coherent whole and as a complement to the volume on Nazi Germany in this series.

A number of central issues and topics are introduced through collections of primary and secondary sources, together with questions of the type likely to be encountered in examinations or other exercises involving use of sources. Practical advice is proffered on the way to approach such questions, and a specimen answer is included.

The selection of sources is very much my own: there is no attempt to aim at any particular 'balance'. For example, the sources on German ambition before and during the First World War may seem to follow a particular trend. This carries no dangers provided that students are aware that any collection is only a partial selection of the evidence in existence, and authors may impose many different criteria for selection, whatever their protestations about 'balance' or 'objectivity'.

Guidance is also offered on the approach to essay questions. Sample essay titles are given with suggestions on relevant approaches; and again, a specimen answer is included.

Finally, an analytical bibliography is intended to give guidance to teachers and students alike.

It is hoped that this collection will prove useful for students working as part of an organised course or on their own.

Thanks are due to Julie Laver, who discussed with me several of the issues raised in this collection and offered useful advice.

APPROACHING SOURCE-BASED

QUESTIONS

Source-based questions have become an important part of History examinations at all levels in recent years. Students who have studied History at GCSE and Standard Grade level will be used to handling various types of sources. The skills they have learned in handling evidence will continue to be applicable at a more advanced level, but there will be more sophisticated skills to master and the sources themselves may be more demanding.

During your studies you will encounter both primary and secondary historical evidence. The distinction between the two is sometimes artificially exaggerated: all sources have their value and limitations, and it is possible to worry unnecessarily about a 'hiearchy of sources'. The important thing for the student is to feel confident in handling all sources. The majority of sources in this book are primary sources, since they are the raw material from which historians work. Many are of a documentary nature, since that is the type most commonly found in examinations. However, there are also statistics and many examples of visual evidence. The comments below will usually apply to *all* types of evidence.

When a student is faced with a piece of historical evidence, there are certain questions that he or she should always ask of that source; but in an examination that student will be asked specific questions set by an examiner and, in the light of pressures, not least of which is time, it is important to approach these questions in an organised and coherent fashion.

The following advice should be borne in mind when answering source-based questions. Some of the advice may appear obvious in the cold light of day but, as examiners will testify, the obvious is often ignored in the cauldron of the examination room!

1 Read the sources carefully before attempting to answer the questions, whether there is one source or a collection of them. This will give you an overview of the sources which will usually be connected and related to a particular theme. You will study the individual sources in detail when you answer specific questions.

2 Always look carefully at the attribution of the sources: the author and date of publication; the recipient, if any; the context in which the source was produced. All these will often give you an insight in addition to that provided by the content of the source itself.

3 Mark allocations are usually given at the end of each question or sub-question. Ignore the marks at your peril! The number of marks will almost certainly give you some indication of the length of answer expected. Length of answer is not an indicator of quality, and there is no such thing as a standard answer, but is is commonplace for candidates in examinations to write paragraph-length answers to questions carrying one or two marks. A question carrying such a low mark can usually be adequately answered in two or three sentences. You do not have the time to waste your purple prose in examinations! Similarly, a mark allocation of nine or ten marks indicates the expectation of a reasonably substantial answer.

4 Study the wording of the questions very carefully. Some questions will ask you to use *only* your own knowledge in the answer; some will ask you to use *both* your own knowledge *and* the source(s); some will insist that you confine your answer to knowledge gleaned from the source(s) *alone*. If you ignore the instructions, you will certainly deprive yourself of marks.

5 If there are several sources to be consulted, ensure that you make use of the ones to which you are directed – candidates have been known to ignore some or choose the wrong ones!

6 Certain types of question require a particular type of response:
a) Comparison and/or contrasting of sources: ensure that you do consider all the sources referred to in the question.
b) Testing the usefulness and limitations of sources: if you are asked to do both, ensure that you do consider both aspects. You may be required to evaluate a source in relation to other information provided, or in the context of your own background knowledge of the subject.
c) Testing reliability. This is not the same as considering the utility of a source, although students sometimes confuse the two concepts.
d) Phrases such as 'Comment upon', 'Analyse' or 'Assess'. Ensure that you do what is asked. Do not be afraid of quoting extracts from a source in your answer, but avoid over-quotation or too much direct paraphrasing. Questions will usually, although not always, be testing more than comprehension, and therefore you should be illustrating or amplifying a particular point. Always *use* the sources and do not just regurgitate what is in front of you.
e) Synthesis: this is a high level skill which requires you to blend several pieces of evidence and draw general conclusions.

7 If at all possible, avoid spending too much time on the sources questions in examinations. Frequently candidates answer the sources questions thoroughly but do not allow themselves enough time to do justice to the rest of the examination paper, and essay answers sometimes suffer in consequence if they are attempted last.

8 If possible, read published examiners' reports which will give you further indication as to the most useful approaches to particular questions, and the pitfalls to avoid.

A Note on this Collection of Sources

It is the intention of this collection to give ideas to teachers and realistic examples of sources and questions to students, either for use in schools and colleges or for self-study purposes. However, they are intended to be flexible. If it is found helpful, adapt the questions or mark allocations, or devise new questions; or use the sources as part of coursework or personal studies. You might even find it an interesting exercise to put together your own sources and appropriate questions!

INTRODUCTION

The Imperial Germany created after the Franco-Prussian War of 1870-1 was in several respects a peculiar creation. It was a federation, but one designed to perpetuate Prussian dominance over other German states. It was a German state which excluded some German-speaking peoples, notably the Austrians, but included French, Danish and Polish minorities.

The political structure created in 1871 was operated relatively smoothly by Bismarck. Although dependent on the Kaiser's favour, like all Imperial Chancellors, Bismarck had the skills and strength of character to make the system work. However, he encountered difficulties in dealing with groups such as Catholics and Socialists and his successors faced several problems in part created by Bismarck himself.

One disturbing factor was the accession of a new Kaiser. Wilhelm II was unstable and impulsive. His interventions in domestic and foreign affairs were rarely constructive, and yet the constitution gave him ultimate power. Bismarck was eased out. Chancellor Caprivi was able, but fell victim to political opponents who persuaded Wilhelm that he himself should and could play a more direct role in government. Caprivi's successor, Hohenlohe, was more compliant but less able. In 1897 von Bülow came to the fore: together with other forceful individuals, notably Tirpitz and Posadowsky, he tried to unite the moderate and conservative political groupings whilst defeating the growing Socialist threat.

Bülow never succeeded in raising the cash necessary to sustain the Kaiser's vision of *Weltpolitik*, which necessitated a vast army, navy and colonial empire. A split with Wilhelm led to the emergence of Bethmann Hollweg in 1909. An able Chancellor, Bethmann nevertheless experienced the same problems of managing insufficient finances and resisting political pressures from both Left and extreme Right. Bethmann was at the helm when Germany entered the First World War in 1914.

1 POLITICAL DEVELOPMENTS

1890-1914

The fundamental political problems of Imperial Germany before 1914 were never resolved: a central government which lacked sufficient clout, based upon a structure designed to ensure Prussia's dominance; a system which gave great power to the Emperor, whilst leaving his Chancellor vulnerable and Parliament with limited powers; the activities of extra-parliamentary pressure groups like the League of Industrialists; the strength of local loyalties which, for example, inhibited the possibility of adequate national taxes; the frequent inability of governments to co-operate with Parliament; the bitter opposition of forces on the Right and Left, with governments often sitting uneasily in the middle.

Did some Germans see war as a way out of a difficult situation? Did certain individuals or groups actively promote war? Was the balance of politics existing before 1914 the same in essence as that which existed until 1930? To what extent did the political parties and forces of these years survive the fall of Imperial Germany in 1918?

A Problems of Government

With the greater independence of the individual departments there is no longer anything to hinder the exaggerated enthusiasm and overweening Prussianism of the bureaucracy . . . He [Caprivi] cannot offer the same degree of opposition to the centralising Privy Councillors as Prince Bismarck could . . . This is not Count Caprivi's fault; it is the fault of the situation itself. Ever since 1870 there has been a basic unclarity, a conflict between particularism and centralism, in our Constitution. This was disguised at first by the personalities of Kaiser Wilhelm I and Prince Bismarck. In future, these contradictions will become ever more noticeable, no matter who is Chancellor.

Report of 8 January 1892, published in A. Brauer *Im Dienste Bismarcks* (Berlin 1936)

B (i) Kaiser Wilhelm II's Views on Governing

Democratic principles can only create weak and often corrupt pillars of society. A society is only strong if it recognises the fact of natural superiorities, in particular that of birth.

Quoted in the *Boston Transcript,* 1882

(ii) The Kaiser on Parliamentary Government

A Prussian Minister is in the fortunate position of not having to worry whether his Bills succeed or not . . . He is not appointed to office at the behest of this or that party in the Chamber. On the contrary, my Ministers are chosen quite freely by me through All-highest confidence; and so long as they enjoy that confidence they do not have to bother about anything else at all. They are, quite simply, better off than they would be in other constitutional States. I should be glad if you would draw the attention of the Ministry to this point from time to time, for in their morally corrupting contact with the Parliaments, one or other of them might be seized with sudden fits of constitutionalism.

Wilhelm II to Hohenlohe, May 1896

(iii) More of the Kaiser's Views

Public opinion didn't concern him. He knew that people didn't love him, and cursed him; but that wouldn't deter him. I then reminded the Emperor of the difference between Prussia and the Empire; said that in Prussia he had old rights which continued to exist, so far as the Prussian Constitution had not limited them. In the Empire the Emperor had only the rights which the Reichstag conceded to him. The Emperor interjected 'the Emperor hardly has any rights', which I attempted to refute. Besides, this was quite unimportant, said HM: the South German democratic states didn't worry him. He had 18 army corps and would make short work of the South Germans.

Report by Hohenlohe, March 1897

C The Basis of Power

I necessarily come to the conclusion that HM must have his natural support among the Conservatives – the Conservatives in the good sense of the word – and this is in line with a glance at Prussian history. For the King of Prussia cannot long remain without the Conservatives . . . I believe, therefore, that the Kaiser's individuality would find its equilibrium in politics on a sensible Conservative basis. The whole of the Kaiser's vital, dynamic being stands in such remarkable contradiction to the predominance of Liberal-Progressive or Liberal-Catholic [Centre] ideas that this has been one of the main reasons for the feeling of unsteadiness about which the whole of Germany is complaining.

Eulenburg to Bülow, 8 June 1896

D The Kaiser's Character

(i) Wilhelm II takes everything personally. Only personal arguments will impress him. He likes to lecture others but will not allow himself to be taught. He cannot bear boredom; heavy-handed, stiff and pedantic people get on his nerves and can achieve nothing through him. Wilhelm

II likes to shine and to do and decide everything by himself . . . To get him to accept an idea one has to pretend that the idea is his own . . . Never forget that HM needs to be praised from time to time . . . You will always achieve all you desire so long as you do not omit to express your admiration whenever HM has earned it.

Eulenberg to Bülow, from Bülow's *Memoirs* (Berlin 1930-31)

(ii) I grow fonder and fonder of the Kaiser. He is so important!! Together with the Great King and the Great Elector he is by far the most important Hohenzollern ever to have lived . . . His vivid imagination lifts me like an eagle high above every petty detail, yet he can soberly judge what is or is not possible and attainable. And what vitality! What a memory! How quick and sure his understanding! In the Crown Council this morning I was completely overwhelmed! He gave an *exposé* of the terribly complicated waterways question – with all that entailed in the way of material and departmental problems – which no departmental Minister could have equalled for precision and accuracy. Yet it was done with a freshness, an attractiveness, a breadth of vision, in short with a brilliance far beyond the reach of any Minister.

Bülow to Eulenberg, 15 February 1898

E Assessments of Kaiser Wilhelm II
(i) In present-day Germany there is no stronger force than the Kaiser. The very complaints of the anti-Kaiser democrats about the growth of personal absolutism are the best proof of this fact, for these complaints are not pure invention but are based on the repeated observation that all policy, foreign and internal, stems from the will and word of the Kaiser. No monarch of absolutist times ever had so much real power as the Kaiser has today. He does not achieve everything he wants, but it is still more than anybody would have believed possible in the middle of the last century.

F. Naumann *Demokratie Und Kaisertum* (Berlin 1900)

(ii) William played a smaller part in the formation of policy than was permitted by the constitution or supposed by the public. Bismarck's departure was undoubtedly his doing, but in the controversies leading to it there was much to be said on the side of the Kaiser, who was in any case only anticipating by a few years the action of natural causes. As regards the failure to renew the Reinsurance Treaty, the Morocco crisis of 1905-6 and the Agadir episode, William was a somewhat unwilling accessory to the acts of other people . . . The only major policy for which prime responsibility must be laid at the Kaiser's door is that regarding the fleet . . . In building such a fleet, William was only carrying to their logical consequence the aspirations of many of his subjects . . .

   This major error points to the main judgement which history must pass on William II. He was a distracting rather than a steadying influence who, instead of helping his Ministers to identify and pursue the ends which really mattered, impeded the cool, objective study of Germany's problems . . . Holding a position in which he could have done much to counterattack the tendencies around him, he instead gave them added emphasis. While claiming to be a leader, he in fact followed others and allowed himself to be moulded by his environment instead of impressing his personality upon it . . .

   William's story demonstrates clearly that good intentions and intelligence are not enough in a ruler. Energy unaccompanied by steadying qualities is a menace rather than an advantage. The effect of charm is apt to be misleading since it does not last. The statesman needs in addition the ability to distinguish the things which matter from the things which seem to matter and the pertinacity to pursue a steady course undistracted by transient excitements . . . The simple truth about the Kaiser is that, for all his undoubted gifts, he was not up to the outsize job which destiny had assigned to him.

M. Balfour *The Kaiser and His Times* (Pelican Books 1975)

Questions

1 What problems facing German Governments are identified in Source A? **(3 marks)**

2 Compare and contrast Wilhelm II's ideas on government as expressed in Sources B (i), B (ii) and B (iii). **(7 marks)**

3 Using your own knowledge, comment upon the accuracy of Eulenburg's assessment of Wilhelm II's position in the political system (Source C). **(5 marks)**

4 Compare and contrast the two assessments of Kaiser Wilhelm II in Source D. **(6 marks)**

5 a What differences are there in the assessments of Kaiser Wilhelm II in Sources E (i) and E (ii)? **(6 marks)**
 b How do you account for any differences? **(4 marks)**

6 Using the evidence of Sources A-E, and your own knowledge, estimate the effectiveness of the Imperial system of Government in Germany between 1890 and 1914. **(12 marks)**

2 ECONOMIC DEVELOPMENTS
1890-1914

By 1890 Germany was already well on the way to asserting itself as the dominant industrial power in Europe. At the same time Germany's agricultural output was also impressive. What were the reasons for Germany's economic strength? There were several relevant factors: fertile land; a large and expanding population, providing a reservoir of workers; an impressive communications network; and a sophisticated banking system which provided ready credit. German business had to import some of the raw materials it required, but had compensating advantages: a large domestic market; and cartel agreements which created monopoly situations. Some industrialists might claim that the German economy would benefit from possession of a large empire, but German industry was already powerful enough to compete successfully with the economies of other countries. This was true even when Government protectionist policies, in the 1880s and again after 1902, provoked retaliatory measures and also had the effect of keeping domestic prices high. The German economy was able to sustain the gigantic military effort made during the First World War. On the other hand, the consequences of Germany's economic drive were not healthy for all sections of the population, either in the countryside or the expanding, crowded cities.

Certain issues may be raised in the context of these developments. How did German society respond to this rapid phase of industrialisation and urbanisation? Was the power of the landowning Junkers affected? How influential were German industrialists as a pressure group? Was the growing importance to the economy of the middle class rewarded with political influence? To what extent was German imperialism economically motivated? What part did economic considerations play in German foreign policy before 1914? What was the relationship between the German political structure and capitalism?

A The German Population (in thousands)

	Total	Males	Females
1890	49,428	24,231	25,198
1900	56,367	27,737	28,630
1910	64,926	32,040	32,886

Census Figures

B The Population of the Five Largest German States (in thousands)

	1871	1880	1890	1900	1910
Prussia	24,689	27,279	29,957	34,473	40,165
Bavaria	4,863	5,285	5,595	6,176	6,887
Saxony	2,556	2,973	3,503	4,202	4,807
Württemburg	1,819	1,971	2,037	2,169	2,438
Baden	1,462	1,570	1,658	1,868	2,143

Census Figures

C The Population of some of the Largest German Towns (in thousands)

	1870/1	1880/1	1890/1	1900/1	1910/1
Berlin	826	1,122	1,579	1,889	2,071
Köln (Cologne)	129	145	282	373	517
Dresden	177	221	277	396	548
Hamburg	240	290	324	706	931
Leipzig	107	149	295	456	590
München (Munich)	169	230	349	500	596

Census Figures

D Birth, Deaths and Marriages in Germany (in thousands)

	Births	Deaths	Marriages
1871	1,414	1,213	337
1880	1,696	1,173	337
1890	1,759	1,199	395
1900	1,996	1,236	476
1910	1,925	1,046	496

Census Figures

E Deaths of Infants Per 1,000 Live Births

1871	330
1880	240
1890	226
1900	229
1910	162

Census Figures

F Occupational Distribution (in thousands)

| | MANUFACTURING | | AGRICULTURE, FORESTRY AND FISHING | |
	Males	Females	Males	Females
1882	3,721	995	5,702	2,535
1895	4,565	1,351	5,540	2,753
1907	5,959	1,875	5,284	4,599

Census Figures

G Index of Industrial Production

1913 = 100

1871	21
1880	49.4
1890	57.3
1990	61
1910	86
1913	100

H Output of Coal in Germany (in thousands of metric tons)

	Hard Coal	Brown Coal	UK Comparison
1871	29,373	8,483	119,235
1880	46,974	12,145	149,327
1890	70,238	19,013	184,528
1900	109,290	40,279	228,794
1910	152,828	69,474	268,676

I Output of Iron Ore in Germany (in thousands of metric tons)

		UK Comparison
1871	3,376	16,902
1880	5,065	18,315
1890	8,047	14,002
1900	12,793	14,253
1910	22,446	15,470

J Output of Crude Steel in Germany (in thousands of metric tons)

		UK Comparison
1871	143	417
1880	690	1,316
1890	2,135	3,636
1900	6,461	4,980
1910	13,100	6,476

K External Trade Aggregate Current Value (millions of marks)

	Imports	Exports
1880	2,814	2,923
1890	4,162	3,335
1900	5,769	4,611
1910	8,927	7,475

L Balance of External Trade with Leading Powers (millions of marks)

I = Imports   E = Exports

	FRANCE		RUSSIA		UK		USA.	
	I	E	I	E	I	E	I	E
1880	246	285	336	213	351	438	-	-
1890	258	231	542	206	601	690	397	417
1900	303	277	717	325	719	862	1,004	440
1910	509	543	1,387	547	767	1,102	1,188	633

M Proportion of German National Product by Sector of Origin (%)

UK Comparison In Brackets

	Agriculture	Industry	Transport And Communications	Commerce
1871	39 (15)	30 (40)	2 (23)	8
1880	36 (15)	32 (40)	3 (24)	8
1890	33 (9)	37 (41)	4 (24)	8
1900	30 (7)	40 (43)	5 (25)	9
1910	25	43	6	9

N German Balance of Payments (millions of marks)

	Visible Balance	Invisible Balance	Overall Current Balance
1880	+120	+168	+288
1890	-819	+1,249	+430
1900	-1,155	+1,566	+411
1910	-1,459	+2,211	+752

O Length of Railway Line in Germany (in kilometres)

		UK Comparison
1871	21,471	21,558
1880	33,838	25,060
1890	42,869	27,827
1900	51,678	30,079
1910	61,209	32,184

P Central Government Expenditure and Revenue in Germany (millions of marks)

	Central Government Expenditure	Total Government Revenue
1871	1,407	(1872) 182
1880	550	294
1890	1,354	661
1900	2,197	887
1910	3,024	1,499

Q Cost of Living Index

1913 = 100

1871	69
1880	76
1890	75
1900	77
1910	92
1913	100

R Economic and Social Concerns

(i) The working class is bound together with industry most intimately, and we would have neglected our duty if we had not, in concluding these treaties, kept the possibility of preserving our working class, preserving their ability to be productive, steadily before us. Two factors then came up for discussion: first, to procure cheaper foodstuffs. In so far as that could take place without endangering state interests . . . the federated governments . . . have effected the lowering of the tariff on foodstuffs which they considered permissible. For the preservation and prosperity of the working class, however, I regard it as far more essential that work should be found for them. (*Quite right! From the Right.*) If this were not the more essential question, then the rush of our rural labourers to the cities and to the West could hardly be explained . . . Remunerative jobs will be found if these treaties are accepted. We will find them by means of export. We must export; either we export goods, or we export people. With this mounting population, and without a comparably growing industry, we are not in a position to survive any longer.

Caprivi speaking about his Trade Treaties in the Reichstag, 1891

(ii) The large landowner wants high grain tariffs and wants to prevent measures of social reform being applied to the countryside, which could make his workers more expensive or demanding. He also does not want to strengthen the peasant proprietor class at the expense of landed property. The heavy industrialist wants a powerful protection for

15

his business, sufficient to secure him the domestic market and enable him to compete in the world market with the surplus of his manufactures. He wants, furthermore, to be master in his own factory, with regard to working conditions and wage levels. If he can regulate the latter, and thereby control the size of his net profit, then agricultural protective tariffs and the consequent increase in production costs are not all that uncomfortable for him.

E. Von Halle *Vols- Und Seewirthschaft: Reden Und Aufsatze* (Berlin 1902)

„Sie haben völlige Freiheit, mein Lieber, Sie können nach rechts oder nach links gehen, ganz wie Sie wollen."

(iii) The choice facing the German worker: one road leads to the factory, the other to prison

Questions

1 What conclusions can be drawn from the Sources A-Q about:

   a Social and economic changes in Germany between 1871 and the First World War? **(12 marks)**

   b Germany's international economic standing? **(5 marks)**

2 **a** What concerns are expressed in Source R (i)-(iii) about Germany's social and economic development? **(7 marks)**

   b Using your own knowledge, and Sources A-R, assess the degree to which these concerns were justified. **(10 marks)**

3 'By 1890, Germany had achieved the decisive shift to an industrial economy . . . But the most pronounced growth and change, and hence social stress, came in the period 1890-1910.' To what extent do Sources A-R support this assertion? **(12 marks)**

3 FOREIGN POLICY

1890-1914

Bismarck's reputations rests partly upon the skill with which he manipulated European alliances during his time as Chancellor. But was German security already on the wane at the time of his fall from power? The Russian link had already been weakened. German policy did not alter decisively immediately after Bismarck's fall. However, Germany's international position deteriorated markedly in the two decades preceding the First World War. Europe appeared to be dividing increasingly into two armed camps; and suspicion of Germany amongst other Powers increased following, for example, her provocative behaviour towards France in the Moroccan crises. Was this suspicion merited? Was it too optimistic to expect German military and naval strength not to provoke forebodings amongst other Great Powers? Wilhelm II's unpredictable and sometimes rash behaviour certainly added to Germany's problems: pushing Britain closer to France was one example.

German foreign policy under Bülow and Bethmann Hollweg was characterised by *Weltpolitik*, a determination to assert a prominent role for Germany in world affairs. Associated with this was a fear of encirclement and a fear of a decline in Germany's international standing. Some prominent Germans even came to the view that a 'preventive' war might be in Germany's interest in 1914. Was there any validity in these fears? A particularly controversial argument is that formulated by the German historian Fischer, that Germany deliberately prompted war in 1914 with world domination in mind. The extent to which Germany was culpable of bringing about war through support of Austria in the crisis of 1914; the country's bellicose behaviour generally; and the extent to which Germany, like other Powers, was simply caught up in the rush to the abyss, characteristic of 'war by timetable' – these are issues of debate among historians. What are your conclusions?

Other contentious issues include: the degree to which internal social, economic and political issues within Germany provoked forward policies as a safety-valve; the influence exerted by military leaders over policy; and the extent to which German Governments simply miscalculated, for example in their estimates of British intentions and capabilities.

Some Germans in powerful positions appeared to believe that a war could best be fought in 1914 rather than two or three years later when other factors might be working against Germany. Does that prove, as the Allied Powers asserted in the Treaty of Versailles in 1919, that Germany and her Allies actually promoted war in 1914? Is the Fischer thesis correct?

A Ideas on Germany's Future Policy

World history is now dominated by the economic struggle. This struggle has raged over the whole globe but most strongly in Europe, where its nature is governed by the fact that central Europe is getting too small and that the free expansion of the peoples who live here is restricted as a result of the present distribution of the inhabitable parts of the earth and above all as a result of the world domination of England . . .

General von Caprivi believed that Germany had no chance at all of becoming a world power, and consequenetly his policy was designed only to maintain Germany's position on the European continent. He was therefore acting quite logically in working at home for the strengthening of the army, limiting the navy to the role of defending the coastline . . . and seeking good relations with England as the natural ally against Russia, the country which threatened Germany's position in Europe.

Caprivi's policy, now so widely ridiculed, would have been brilliantly vindicated by history if the German people were not coming to accept an entirely different opinion of their ability and duty to expand than that expressed in our naval and colonial development so far.

Here, too, our motto must be all or nothing. Either harness the total strength of the nation, ruthlessly, even if it means accepting the risk of a major war, or we limit ourselves to continental power alone . . .

Now, the Caprivi policy has been officially abandoned, and the new Reich Government will hesitantly put to the nation the question – in the form of the new Navy Bill – whether the other policy, *Weltpolitik*, really can be adopted. Let us hope that this question receives an enthusiastic 'Yes' for an answer, but also that then a change comes over our external relations in favour of an understanding with England, beside which there is still a lot of room on this earth which is empty or could be made empty and against whose goodwill even a quite different naval development from the one that now appears to be envisaged would not be sufficient to pursue *Weltpolitik*, in spite of Russia's friendship.

Memorandum by Admiral Georg Von Müller, 1896 (written for Kaiser Wilhelm II's brother)

B Bülow's Ideas on Foreign Policy

Only a successful external policy can help, reconcile, pacify, rally, unite. Its preconditions are of course caution, patience, tact, reflection . . . It is not a good idea to sound a victory fanfare before the definitive victory, excessive sabre-rattling annoys without frightening. The main thing remains steadiness and a sense of proportion i.e. neither offending foreign powers – Russia as well as Britain – unnecessarily, nor making them insolent by all too lively advances.

Bülow to Eulenburg, 1897

19

C Caricature and Propaganda

(i) A French Cartoon shows Wilhelm II as a one-man band in Europe

(ii) The growth of German naval power worries England in this German cartoon. King Edward VII says to his nephew, the Kaiser: 'Your little masterpiece is too ambitious, keep it as a sketch.'

D Pan-Germanism

(i) We reckon 60 million souls in the German Reich, and approximately 30 million German-speaking people abroad. This colossal mass, linked by ties of blood and language, must be bound together and ever more intimately embraced by ethical, literary and economic interests. That is how 'the Greater German Reich', of which our Emperor spoke as early as 1896, must be formed . . .

When all Germans are convinced of the truth and importance of these principles . . . then there will be a stirring of that self-consciousness and national pride which is as yet absent in our people. Then the German people will occupy among the other nations the place that is due to them by virtue of their inner worth.

General E. Von Liebert *Ziele Der Deutschen Kolonial- Und Auswanderungspolitik* (1907)

Germany and areas for
future German influence

Rußland

England

• Warschau

Deutschland   Polen

Paris •

Frankreich

Rumänien
Sarajevo   • Budapest
Serbien   Bulgarien
Italien   Sofia
Madrid   *Deutschland*
•
Spanien   Athens
Albanien   Griechenland

Marokko   Tunis
Deutsch   Algier
Tripolis –   England
Italien

**(ii) 'Europe in 1950 – A Continental and Mediterranean Great-
Germany Map', based on Dr O. R. Tannenberg *Grossdeutschland –
Die Arbeit Des 20ten Jahrhunderts* (Leipzig 1911)**

**(Germany and potential German territorial aims are indicated in
grey.)**

E Germany and the Next War

(i) If we do not decide for war, that war in which we shall have to engage at the latest in two or three years will be begun in far less propitious circumstances. At this moment the initiative rests with us; Russia is not ready, moral factors and right are on our side, as well as might. Since we have to accept the conflict some day, let us provoke it at once. Our prestige, our position as a Great Power, our honour are in question and yet more, for it would seem that our very existence is threatened.

The *German Military Review,* July 1909

(ii) We have fought in the last great wars for our national union and our position among the powers of Europe; we must now decide whether we wish to develop into and maintain a world empire, and procure for German spirit and German ideas that fit recognition which has been hitherto withheld from them.

Have we the energy to aspire to that great goal? Are we prepared to make the sacrifices which such an effort will doubtless cost us? Or are we willing to recoil before the hostile forces, and sink step by step lower in our economic, political and national importance? That is what is involved in our decision . . .

We must make it quite clear to ourselves that there can be no standing still, no being satisfied for us, but only progress or retrogression, and that is tantamount to retrogression when we are contented with our present place among the nations of Europe, while all our rivals are straining with desperate energy, even at the cost of our rights, to extend their power. The process of our decay would set in gradually and advance slowly so long as the struggle against us was waged with peaceful weapons; the living generation would, perhaps, be able to continue to exist in peace and comfort. But should a war be forced upon us by stronger enemies under conditions unfavourable to us, then, if our arms met with disaster, our political downfall would not be delayed, and we should rapidly sink down. The future of German nationality would be sacrificed, an independent German civilisation would not long exist, and the blessings for which German blood has flowed in streams – spiritual and moral liberty, and the profound and lofty aspirations of German thought – would for long ages be lost to mankind.

If, as is right, we do not wish to assume the responsibility for such a catastrophe, we must have the courage to strive with every means to attain that increase of power which we are entitled to claim, even at the risk of a war with numerically superior foes.

Under the present conditions it is out of the question to attempt this by acquiring territory in Europe. The region in the east, where German colonists once settled, is lost to us, and could only be recovered from

Russia by a long and victorious war, and would then be a perpetual incitement to renewed wars. So, again, the re-annexation of the former South Prussia, which was united to Prussia on the second partition of Poland, would be a serious undertaking, on account of the Polish population.

Under these circumstances we must clearly try to strengthen our political power in other ways.

In the first place, our political position would be considerably consolidated if we could finally get rid of the standing danger that France will attack us on a favourable occasion, as soon as we find ourselves involved in complications elsewhere. In one way or another we must square our account with France if we wish for a free hand in our international policy. This is the first and foremost condition of a sound German policy, and since the hostility of France once and for all cannot be removed by peaceful overtures, the matter must be settled by force of arms. France must be so completely crushed that she can never again come across our path.

Friedrich Von Bernhardi *Deutschland Und Der Nachste Krieg* (Stuttgart-Berlin 1913)

F The Kaiser's Verdict

Frivolity and weakness are going to plunge the world into the most frightful war of which the ultimate object is the overthrow of Germany. For I no longer have any doubt that England, Russia and France have *agreed* among themselves – knowing that our treaty obligations compel us to support Austria – to use the Austro-Serb conflict as a *pretext* for waging a war of annihilation against us. That is the explanation of Grey's cynical remark . . . that 'as long as the war is confined to Russia and Austria, England will sit still, and only when we and France get ourselves *mixed up* with it will he be forced to take active steps against us'. That means we are either basely to betray our ally and *leave her to the mercy of Russia* – thereby breaking up the Triple Alliance, or as a reward for keeping our *pledges* get set upon and *beaten* by the Triple Entente in a body, so that their longing to *ruin* us completely can be finally satisfied. That is in a nutshell the bare bones of the situation, slowly but surely brought about by Edward VII; carried forward systematically by the secret conversations in Paris and St Petersburg, the occurrence of which England has always denied; finally completed and put into operation by George V . . . So the celebrated *encirclement* of Germany has finally become an accomplished fact, in spite of all the efforts by our politicians to prevent it . . . We fell into the net and started to build only one capital ship a year in the pious hope that we would thereby reassure England! All requests and warnings on my part went unregarded. Now we get what the English consider to be gratitude. Our dilemma over keeping faith with the old and honourable Emperor has been exploited to create a situation which gives England the excuse she has been seeking to annihilate us with a spurious appearance of justice on the pretext that she is helping France and maintaining the well-known Balance of Power in Europe, i.e. playing off all European States for her own benefit against us.

Comments by Wilhelm II on a Report, July 1914

G A Modern Historian's Verdict

Contemplating the self-restraint of the Bismarckian and Caprivi eras with a mixture of pity and contempt, and partly animated by concern that the British might go over to protectionism and close off her markets, a younger generation of Germans unleashed on all parts of the globe a hectic flurry of activity known as 'World policy', seeking to gain spheres of influence in China, for example, in South America, in Turkey especially, and, above all, additional colonies in Africa and the Pacific. What this amounted to in the consciousness of the nation, among the so-called liberal imperialists in particular, was a redivision of the globe that would more accurately reflect prevailing power relations, i.e. acknowledge the rise of the German Empire, than did the status quo. In practice, this could be attained only by means of war . . .

After 1905 the Reich attempted, in a number of major crises, to break out of its 'encirclement', invariably doing so with an eye to the probable domestic ramifications. Its final endeavour led to the First World War. During these crises the Kaiser repeatedly revealed his own weakness. When he again 'caved in' on 28 July 1914 he was pushed aside. In all this, and at the crux of military deliberations from 1908 onwards, there was the anticipated and accepted two-front war with France and Russia. Only the active hostility of the third world power, Britain, remained in doubt . . .

In reality, there did indeed exist at the summit of the Reich a degree of collaboration between political and military leaders, embracing propagandist and psychological as well as financial and economic preparations for war. A clear decision was made to secure and extend its European base, although, with a view to Britain, the timetable, tactics and line of march might vary. And this decision was taken not from a purely military standpoint to secure a Great Power's 'freedom of action' because in 1916-17 French and Russian counter-measures would be complete; it was made from a long-term power-political, economic and domestic political perspective . . .

The German military leaders' confidence in victory was based on the Moltke-Schlieffen doctrine of the short war, in accordance with the tradition of the wars of 1864, 1866 and 1870. It was dominated by the pre-eminence of operational thought over a realistic assessment of the numerical strength and resources of the opponent and of one's own long-term potentialities.

F. Fischer *From Kaiserreich To Third Reich* (English edition Unwin Hyman 1986)

Questions

1 What arguments are used in Source A to justify a forward foreign policy for Germany? **(4 marks)**

2 To what extent does Source B support the arguments in Source A? **(5 marks)**

3 What are the uses and limitations of the cartoons in Source C to an historian studying German foreign policy in this period? **(6 marks)**

4 Compare Sources D (i) and (ii) as evidence of pan-Germanism in this period. **(7 marks)**

5 How reliable is Source E (i) for an understanding of German foreign policy before the First World War? **(4 marks)**

6 **a** Identify elements of propaganda in Source E (ii). **(4 marks)**
   b Comment upon the value of Sources E (ii) and F as evidence for an understanding of the origins of the First World War. **(8 marks)**

7 Using your own knowledge, explain the phrase 'Moltke-Schlieffen doctrine of short war' in Source G (line 33) **(5 marks)**

8 To what extent does the evidence of Sources A-F confirm the arguments of Fischer in Source G? **(10 marks)**

4 GERMANY AND THE
FIRST WORLD WAR

Germany underwent at least one similar experience to that of the other Great Powers involved in the First World War: that is, an initial enthusiasm, almost euphoria, for what was considered a just cause – defence against unprovoked attack. However, the near-unanimous support for the Government and Army lasted longer in Germany than in some participating countries. Even the Social Democrats, who supposedly put internationalism before narrow patriotic duty, rallied to the war effort.

Perhaps it was inevitable that the protracted character of the war produced changes. One was increasing military control over the Government; by 1916 Hindenburg and Ludendorff were deciding policy and even appointments. Another development was increasing Government interference in, and control over, the economy, although rapid inflation demonstrated the Government's inability to cope successfully with the financial demands of the war, whatever the strength of the German economy.

The debilitating effects of a long war took their toll. The military distrusted Bethmann Hollweg and he was finally forced out of office in July 1917. The Social Democrats at last called for a compromise peace, but the grip of the military seemed stronger than ever.

The internal situation changed dramatically in 1918 with the failure of Germany's last offensive and American entry into the War. For the first time, German civilians began to learn about the real situation and the effects of the war on Germany. When morale in the Army was no longer certain, its leaders finally came round. A parliamentary monarchy was set up to negotiate an ending to the war. Revolution at Kiel in November 1918 hurried events further, leading to the abdication of the Kaiser, fears of a Left-wing coup, and the signing of the Armistice.

Emotive issues arose out of the experience of the war years. The publication of German war aims symbolised the ambitious expectations of German nationalists. The Treaty of Brest-Litovsk, forced upon the Russian Government, showed how far they were prepared to go.

Can subsequent German history only be understood in the context of the war experience? Was the bringing to the fore of strong nationalist claims, notably in Eastern Europe, a foreshadowing of the Nazi era? To what extent were Germans psychologically shaken by defeat and its consequences? Hunger, fear and disillusionment were rife; and political parties were divided. The Weimar Republic, succeeding the Kaiser's Germany, was born in the most unpropitious circumstances. Did this fact determine its subsequent fate?

A War Propaganda

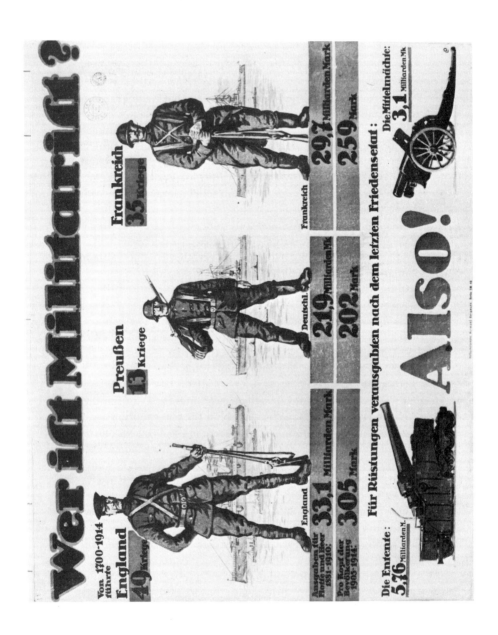

'Who is Militaristic?' – A German poster compares Germany's past
record in wars with those of Britain and France

B The Social Democrats State Their Position

We Social Democrats in this solemn hour are at one with the whole German nation, without distinction of party or creed, in accepting the fight forced upon us by Russian barbarism, and we are ready to fight till the last drop of blood for Germany's national independence, fame and greatness.

Der Volksfreund, Karlsruhe, 1 August 1914

C Bethmann Hollweg Speaks

A tremendous fate has fallen upon Europe. While we have endeavoured to maintain the prestige of the German Empire in the eyes of the world, we have lived for 44 years in peace and protected European peace. In this work of peace we have become strong and mighty – therefore we are envied. We have suffered with long-enduring patience, while in the East and West, under the excuse that Germany is lusting for war, hatred for us has been nourished and fetters wrought wherewith to bind us. The wind which blows there has now become a storm.

We desired nothing but to live on in peaceful toil, content with an unspoken oath that was echoed from the Emperor down to the youngest recruit. Our sword shall only leap from its sheath in defence of a just cause. (*Loud applause*). . .

We are now in a position of self defence, and necessity knows no law! (*Cries of* 'Quite right') Our troops have occupied Luxembourg, perhaps they have already entered Belgium. (*Loud applause*) That is a breach of international law. The French Government, it is true, had declared in Brussels that they would respect Belgian neutrality so long as their opponent respected it. But we knew that France stood ready to invade it. (*Cries of indignation*)

France could wait, we could not, and a French attack on our flank on the Lower Rhine might have been disastrous for us. Thus we were compelled to ignore the protests of the Luxembourg and Belgian Governments.

The injustice which we commit thereby, we shall try to make good again as soon as our military goal is attained. Anyone who fights for the highest, as we do now, may only think of how he may hack his way through.
(*Hurricanes of applause, long-continued hand-clapping in the whole house and on the tribune*)

Gentlemen, so much for events up till now! I repeat the words of the Kaiser: 'We enter the struggle with a clear conscience!' (*Great enthusiasm*) . . . The hour of great trial has struck for our nation. But we look forward to it with absolute confidence. (*Tremendous applause*)

Our army is in the field, our fleet is ready, and behind them the entire German nation (*roars of enthusiastic applause and hand-clapping in the whole House*) – the whole German nation! (*These words were accompanied by a gesture towards the Social Democrats – Renewed outburst of applause, in which the Social Democrats also joined*)

Gentlemen, you know your duty in its entirety. The vote of credit requires no further argument, I beg you to pass it quickly. (*Loud applause*)

Chancellor Bethmann Hollweg in the Reichstag, 4 August 1914

D Justifications for Germany's Actions

(i) Let us renounce our miserable efforts to excuse Germany, let us cease to hurl contemptible insults at the enemy. It is not against our will that we are now thrown into this gigantic adventure. It has not been thrust upon us by surprise. We have wished it; we must wish it. We do not appear before the tribunal of Europe; we do not recognise any such jurisdiction . . .

Look! Is Germany strong? Yes. What are you muttering then, bespectacled professors and carpet-slippered theologians? That there is such a thing as right? That noble ideas have any value? What chimeras are you seeking to defend? One principle alone counts, one alone which summarises and contains all the others: force. Demand that, and away with the nonsense! Force, there is the word which sounds loud and clear, which has style and allure. Force, a fist, that is everything!

Maximilian Harden *Zukunft* (1914)

(ii) O Germany, hate! Slaughter thy millions of adversaries and build a monument of smoking corpses which rise up to the clouds.

O Germany, hate now! Gird thyself with brass and with thy bayonet pierce the heart of every enemy; take no prisoners! Render them all mute; transform the neighbouring countries into deserts . . . Battalions, batteries, squadrons, all forward! Afterward thou wilt review them on the ruins of the world, healed for ever of thine ancient folly, of thy love for foreigners.

Poem by Heinrich Vierordt (1914)

(iii) As representatives of Science and Art, we hereby protest to the civilised world against the lies and calumnies with which our enemies are endeavouring to stain the honour of Germany in her hard struggle for existence – in a struggle which has been forced upon her . . .

It is not true that Germany is guilty of having caused this war. Neither the people, the Government, nor the Kaiser, wanted war. Germany did her utmost to prevent it . . .

It is not true that we trespassed in neutral Belgium. It has been proved that France and England had resolved on such a trespass, and it has likewise been proved that Belgium had agreed to their doing so. It would have been suicide on our part not to have been beforehand . . .

It is not true that our warfare pays no respect to international laws. It knows no undisciplined cruelty. But in the East the earth is saturated with the blood of women and children unmercifully butchered by the wild Russian troops, and in the West dum-dum bullets mutilate the breasts of our soldiers. Those who have allied themselves with Russians and Serbians, and present such a shameful scene to the world as that of inciting Mongolians and Negroes against the white race, have no right whatever to call themselves upholders of civilisation . . .

Have faith in us. Believe that we shall carry on this war to the end as a civilised nation, to whom the legacy of a Goethe, a Beethoven, and a Kant is just as sacred as its own hearths and homes.

Manifestio signed by 93 German Professors and other Intellectuals, published in the USA on 10 October, 1914

(iv) If Jesus of Nazareth, who preached the love of enemies, were again among us in the flesh – nowehere would he rather be incarnate than in Germany – where do you think he would be found? Do you think he would be standing in a pulpit and saying angrily: 'You sinful Germans, love your enemies'? Certainly not. Instead, he would be right in front, in the first ranks of the sword-bearers who are fighting with implacable hatred. This is where he would be, and he would bless the bleeding hands and the death-dealing weapons, would perhaps himself grasp a sword of judgement and drive the enemies of the Germans farther and farther from the frontiers of the Promised Land, as he once drove the Jewich merchants and usurers out of the Temple.

R. H. Heybrodt *'Im Deutschen Wald' Volkserzieher*, 1915

E The National Liberal Attitude
The Executive of the National Liberal Party emphatically reiterates its conviction, expressed on 15 August 1915 and since confirmed by events, that only an extension of the land and sea boundaries of Germany's sphere of power in the East and West and overseas can furnish the necessary real guarantees to the German people for its future military, political and economic security.

Resolution passed in Berlin by the Executive of the National Liberal Party, 21 May 1916

F A Dissenting View
(i) The time I spent in the stranglehold of militarism was a period of constant resistance – and I know there was not one thing I did which did not utterly disgust me . . .

Maps Showing the German Government's War Aims

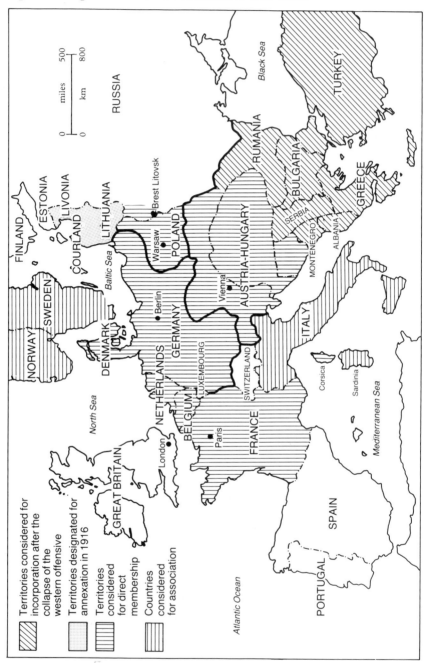

(i) **Bethmann Hollweg's Programme of September 1914: 'Central Europe as a new economic unit'**

32

(ii) The German 'New Order' in the East, 1914-18

I have one dream: perhaps there will, after all, be changes, rebellions – perhaps one day international socialism which has lost its backbone will gather strength enough for an open uprising – and then W. II and the Crown Prince – it is an absurd dream, no more – . . . to the slaughterhouse!

Letter from the Artist George Grosz to Robert Bell, September 1915 (Grosz was discharged from the Germany Army in May 1915, because of illness)

(ii) It is true that I am opposed to war: that is to say I am opposed to any system that coerces me. From an aesthetic point of view, on the other hand, I rejoice over every German who dies a hero's death on the field of honour (how touching!). To be a German means invariably to be crude, stupid, ugly, fat and inflexible – it means to be unable to climb up a ladder at forty, to be badly dressed – to be a German means: to be a reactionary of the worst kind; it means only one amongst a hundred will, occasionally, wash all over.

Letter from George Grosz to Robert Bell, 1916

G The Home Front

(i) Your Excellency knows what tremendous tasks face our munition industry if a successful result of the war is to be attained. The decisive factor is the solution of the labour problem, not only as regards the numbers of workpeople, but specially as regards the provision of ample food to enable each individual to put forth his maximum effort . . . It does not seem to me to be sufficiently recognised everywhere among the officials that the existence or non-existence of our people and Empire is at stake . . . It is impossible for our working people to maintain their full strength if they do not succeed in obtaining a sufficient supply of fat, allotted to them on a proper basis . . .

I beg your Excellency most urgently to impress upon all Federal Governments, administrative and communal authorities, the seriousness of the situation, and to demand that they shall use every means to provide sufficient nourishment for our munition workers, and unite all the leading men of all parties as leaders of the Army at home behind the plough and the lathe to work together and arouse the *furor Teutonicus* among the tillers of the soil as well as among the townspeople and munition workers.

Letter from German Chief of Staff Hindenburg to the Chancellor, 27 September 1916

(ii) The German people are feeling the pinch of war. The lack of butter, bread and other necessary commodities is severely felt. But the people are far too disciplined to do more than grumble, for a long time to come.

The result of the war is not in doubt, but the Allies must be prepared for a protracted and sullen resistance on the part of Germany, and ought not to underestimate the difficulty of wearing down the spirit of a people which, after all, is profoundly patriotic and schooled to accept with fatalistic resignation the decisions of its Government.

The word 'fatalism' best expresses the mood of Germany today. Warlike enthusiasm has gone. Hope of a sweeping victory has departed, but nothing justifies the supposition that the German masses are likely to revolt against the authorities for many a long day. The Allies must therefore redouble their efforts to render the blockade increasingly stringent, and make up their minds to the fact that, though half beaten, Germany is far from recognising in practice the hopelessness of her plight.

Times History of the War, Volume 9, recording an account given by the Portugese Ambassador in Berlin in 1916

(iii) When the conduct of operations was entrusted to me [Hindenburg was appointed Commander of the Armed Forces in 1916] I regarded the country's morale as serious, though it had not collapsed. There was no doubt that people at home had been bitterly disappointed by the military events of the last few months. Moreover, the privations of daily life had materially increased. The middle classes in particular were suffering very severely from the economic situation, which affected them exceptionally intensely. Food had become very scarce, and the prospects of the harvest were only moderate.

P. Von Hindenburg *Out of My Life* (London 1920)

(iv) In the middle of August [1918] I did not consider that the time had come for us to despair of a successful conclusion of the war. In spite of certain distressing but isolated occurrences in the last battle, I certainly hoped that the Army would be in a position to continue to hold out. I also believed that our public at home would be strong enough to survive even the present crisis. I fully realised what the homeland had already borne in the way of sacrifices and privations and what they would possibly still have to bear. Had not France, on whose soil the war had now been raging for four years, had to suffer and endure far more? Had that country ever been cast down by failure during the whole of that time? Did she despair when our shells fell into her capital? I believed that our own public would keep this in mind even in this serious crisis, and stand firm if only we at the front continued to stand firm too.

P. Von Hindenburg *Out of My Life* (London 1920)

H Reflections on the Outcome

The proud German Army, after victoriously resisting an enemy superior in numbers for four years, performing feats unprecedented in history, and keeping our foes from our frontiers, disappeared in a moment. Our victorious fleet was handed over to the enemy. The authorities at home, who had not fought against the enemy, could not hurry fast enough to pardon deserters and other military criminals, including among these many of their own number, themselves and their nearest friends.

They and the Soldiers' Councils worked with zeal, determination and purpose to destroy the whole military structure. Such was the gratitude of the new homeland to the German soldiers who had bled and died for it in millions. The destruction of Germany's power to defend herself – the work of Germans – was the most tragic crime the world has witnessed. A tidal wave had broken over Germany, not by the force of nature, but through the weakness of the Government, represented by the Chancellor, and the paralysis of a leaderless people.

E. Ludendorff *War Memories* (London 1933 ed.)

Questions

1 How does the author of Source A attempt to convey its message?

(4 marks)

2 In what ways does Bethmann Hollweg attempt to justify Germany's participation in the war (Source C)? **(6 marks)**

3 Compare and contrast Sources B, C, D (i), (ii), (iii), (iv), and E as propaganda in support of Germany's cause in the First World War.

(12 marks)

4 What are the uses and limitations of the maps on pages 32 and 33 as evidence of Germany's war aims in the First World War? **(7 marks)**

5 What was George Grosz's opinion of Germany and the War (Source F)? **(4 marks)**

6 Study Source G:
   a What problems for Germany on the Home Front are identified in these four extracts? **(7 marks)**
   b Do these extracts suggest that Germany's defeat was inevitable?

(5 marks)

   c How would you test the reliability of any one of the four extracts in Source G? **(4 marks)**

7 Using your own knowledge, assess the truth of Ludendorff's accusations in Source H. **(5 marks)**

8 In 1919 the Allies blamed Germany both for causing the War and for the 'savage and inhuman' way in which it was conducted; and some historians have claimed that Germany harboured ambitious war aims. To what extent can Sources A-H in this Unit and the maps on pages 32 and 33 be used to support or refute those assertions? **(12 marks)**

5 CRISIS AND CONSTITUTION

Well before the revolution of November 1918 there were signs of anti-war feeling and political unrest. The majority Social Democratic leadership (SPD) were brought into the Government in an attempt to avert Left-wing revolution and possibly to persuade the Allies that the German Establishment had changed its political complexion and was worthy of moderate peace terms. The SPD's reward was to be reviled by the breakaway Independent Social Democrats (USPD) and other radical groups for selling out; whilst the conservative establishment regarded them cynically as an expedient, to be used in its own interests and then discarded. The moderate Socialists never satisfactorily resolved the dilemma of their position. This position was made more difficult by the fact that as prominent members of the new Government, the Socialists had to face momentous difficulties such as the creation of a new constitution and the signing of what was widely regarded as a humiliating peace settlement.

The Constitution of the Weimar Republic, adopted in July 1919, satisfied no-one entirely. Several issues were not satisfactorily resolved, and potential problems were created: the role of the President, and the relationship between the Reich Government and the States (Länder). The technicalities of the Constitution were one thing; problems caused by coalition politics and intercinine party conflicts were another.

Perhaps of more immediate concern was the very survival of the Republic. It was under threat from destructive impulses on the Left (for example the Spartacists) and the Right (the Kapp Putsch). The early years of the Republic were literally a battleground.

Several questions and issues emerge from a study of these early years of crisis and instability. Was there in fact a Revolution? If so, did it change very much in Germany? Did the circumstances in which the Weimar Republic emerged effectively prevent it from having any real long-term chance of success? Was it only the efforts of Left and Right extremists to discredit and destroy the Republic, already in evidence in the early years, that precluded stability? Did the early struggles and problems divide and weaken society and open the way later to the Nazis? Did the Weimar Republic ever have or deserve a real chance? How many Germans even believed in the democracy and social contract enshrined in the Constitution?

A Karl Liebknecht on the German Revolution

I am afraid that I must try to pour cold water on your enthusiasm. The counter-revolution is already on the march; it is already in action! (*Shouts: 'Where is that?'*) It is already among us. Those who have spoken to you, were they friends of the revolution? (*Shouts: 'No!' Loud retorts: 'Yes!'*) Read what Reich Chancellor Ebert (*Shout: 'Without him you would not even be here!'*) had printed in *Vorwärts.* It is a slander of the revolution carried out yesterday.

Dangers to the revolution threaten us from many sides. (*Shouts: 'From you!'*) Danger threatens not only from those circles that up to now have held the reins – the demagogues, big landowners, junkers, capitalists, imperialists, monarchists, princes, and generals – but also from those who today support the revolution, but were still opposing it the day before yesterday. (*Stormy interruptions: 'Unity, unity!' Retorts: 'No!' Shouts: 'Sit down!'*)

Be careful whom you choose for the government and whom you trustingly elect to the soldiers' councils. The soldiers' councils must be in the vanguard of the defence of the councils' power. No significant portion of the councils' power can be placed in the hands of officers. The reins must be primarily in the hands of the simple soldiers. (*Loud shouts: 'They are!'*) In the provinces several higher officers have been elected chairmen of soldier's councils. (*Protests*) I tell you: Enemies surround us! (*Shouts: 'You're twisting the facts!'*) The revolution's enemies are insidiously using the soldier's organisations to their own ends. (*Persistent commotion*) I know how unpleasant this disturbance is, but even if you shoot me, I will say what I believe to be necessary. The triumph of the revolution will be possible only if it becomes a social revolution. Only then will it have the strength to ensure the socialisation of the economy, happiness, and peace for all eternity. (*Applause from some, peristent uproar, renewed shouts: 'Unity!'*)

Speech by Karl Liebknecht at SPD/USPD Meeting in Berlin, 10 November 1918

B The Social Democrats and Communism

It was hunger that forced the Russian people under the yoke of militarism. Russia's workers went on strike, destroyed the economy through overhasty socialisation, deprived themselves of the means of making a living through unrealisable demands, and sacrificed their freedom to militarism. Bolshevik militarism is the violent despotism of a clique, the dictatorship of the idlers and those unwilling to work. Russia's army, made up of masses of unemployed workers, is today already waging another bloody war.

Let the Russian example be a warning. Do we also want another war? Do we want terror, the bloody reign of a caste?

NO!

We want no more bloodshed and no militarism. We want to achieve peace through work. We want peace, in order not to degenerate into a militarism dictated by the unemployed, as in Russia. Bolshevik bums call the armed masses into the streets, and armed masses, bent on violence, are militarism personified. But we do not want militarism of the right or of the left.

Bolshevism, the lazy man's militarism, knows no freedom or equality. It is vandalism and terror by a small group that arrogates power. So do not follow Spartacus, the German Bolsheviks, unless you want to ruin our economy and trade.

The collapse of German industry and trade means the downfall of the German people.

So, no to terror, not to militaristic rule by loafers and deserters.

Not militarism, but *freedom!*

Article in the SPD Newspaper *Vorwärts*, 24 December 1918

C A Liberal View from 1918

The middle class is frightened and at its wits' end, not knowing what to do or where to turn; most of them are fluttering like birds who have fallen out of the nest and do not know where to go . . . Social Democracy and Catholicism are incontestably two forces of immense importance, and at present the two of the greatest importance. They not only have great hosts at their back but are now the only compact and well knit bodies in the country. But Germany is Germany and anybody with his eyes open and able to look ahead cannot accept these two strong pillars as enough in the long run to give the needed support to a republic – for the Republic has become the only possible thing. Whether it will have a long life in any case is impossible to say as yet, but if at birth it has only a Social Democratic and a Catholic godfather it will be burdened from the outset with a mass of discontent and hostility, and it will be discredited for almost all who might be won over to it from other camps. Thus it is necessary now to organise those strata of the non-Catholic middle-class who are at all inclined towards democratic ideas.

T. Wolff *Through Two Decades* (Heinemann 1936)

D The Spartacist Programme

The National Assembly is an outdated legacy of the bourgeois revolutions, an empty shell, a stage prop from the time of petty-bourgeois illusions of a 'united people', of the bourgeois state's 'liberty, equality, fraternity' . . .

The question today is not democracy or dictatorship. The question that history has put on the agenda reads: *bourgeois* democracy or *socialist* democracy. For the dictatorship of the proletariat is democracy in the socialist sense of the word. Dictatorship of the proletariat does not mean bombs, putsches, riots and anarchy, as the agents of capitalist profits deliberately and falsely claim. Rather it means using all instruments of political power to achieve socialism, to expropriate the capitalist class, through and in accordance with the will of the revolutionary majority of the proletariat.

Manifesto by Rosa Luxemburg

E The Spartacist Rising
Worker, Soldier, Citizen!

Today at one o'clock 3,000 men with heavy artillery and machine guns marched through Berlin and Charlottenburg. Through them the Government showed that it has the power to carry out your will, which demands an end to the pillaging and bloodshed.

Today the Government still hopes that your firm determination will *intimidate terrorism*, that the Spartacists will not launch a fight for the stolen buildings, but will instead vacate their shameful showcases.

Should the hope be dashed that, at the last moment, they will come to their senses, *then the Government's and your patience will be exhausted.* You must chase them out if they delay even one day. In the east, Spartacist gangs drive from house to house plundering with drawn revolvers while Eichhorn's police force stands watch. The charade that this is a political movement has been exposed.

Robbery and plunder are revealed as the ultimate and single goal of the rioters.

Workers!

The Reich government has entrusted me with the leadership of the republican soldiers.

This means that a worker stands at the peak of power in the socialist republic.

You know me and my history in the party. I promise that no unnecessary blood will be spilled.

I am to cleanse, not to destroy.

With the new republican army, I want to bring you freedom and peace.

The working class must stand united against Spartacus, if democracy and socialism are not to be lost.

Declaration by SPD Minister of Defence, Noske, January 1919

F Counter-Revolutionary Measures

(i) G. Grosz: *The Communists are dying and the foreign exchange rate goes up*, 1920. Grosz links military action against the workers with the economic interests of the ruling classes.

(ii) G. Grosz: *Knocking-off time*, 1920. The Reichswehr soldier leans against a tree after a hard day.

G The Kapp Putsch

The Reich and nation are in grave danger. With terrible speed we are approaching the complete collapse of the State and of law and order. The people are only dimly aware of the approaching disaster. Prices are rising unchecked. Hardship is growing. Starvation threatens. Corruption, usury, nepotism and crime are cheekily raising their heads. The Government, lacking in authority, impotent, and in league with corruption, is incapable of overcoming the danger . . .

From the east we are threatened by destruction and violation by war-like Bolshevism. Is this Government capable of resisting it? How are we to escape internal and external collapse?

Only by re-erecting a strong State . . . there is no other way but a government of action.

What are the tasks facing this new government? . . .

The Government will
ruthlessly suppress strikes and sabotage . . . striking is treason to the nation, the Fatherland and the future.

The Government will
. . . not be a one-sided capitalist one. It will rather save German work from the hard fate of slavery to international big business and hopes by such measures to put an end to the hostility of the working classes to the State . . .

We shall govern not according to theories but according to the practical needs of the State and the nation as a whole. In the best German tradition the State must stand above the conflict of classes and parties. It is the objective arbiter in the present conflict between capital and labour. We reject the granting of class-advantage either to the Right or the Left. We recognise only German citizens . . .

Everyone must do his duty! The first duty of every man today is to work. Germany must be a moral working community!

The colours of the German Republic are
Black-White-Red!

The Reich Chancellor
Kapp

Proclamation by Wolfgang Kapp, 13 March 1920

H The Electoral Bases of Some Left and Right Wing Parties in Germany between 1912 and 1920/2

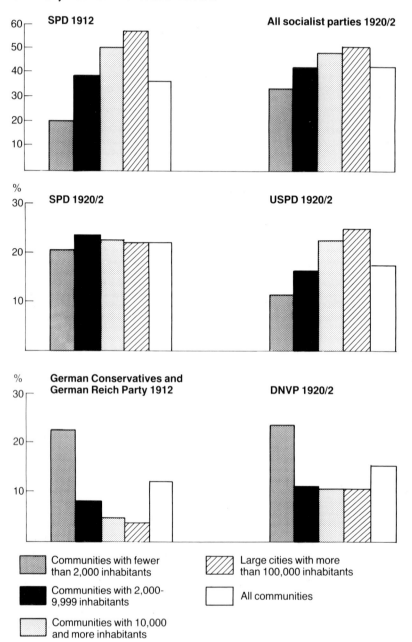

From data in *Statistik Des Deutschen Reichs* vol 250, 1912/13, and vol 291, 1920-3

I The SPD Programme

The Social Democratic Party of Germany is the *party of the working people* in town and country . . . *It considers the democratic republic to be the form of government irrevocably given by historical development*, and it regards every assault upon it as an attempt on the vital rights of the people . . . It is fighting for the supremacy of the people's will, organised in the free people's state, over the economy and for the *renewal of society in the spirit of Socialist solidarity* . . . It is fighting not for new class privileges and prerogatives but for the *abolition of class rule* and of class itself and for equal rights and equal obligations for all without distinction of sex and origin.

In that campaign it makes the following demands: . . .

National state control of the capitalist ownership of the means of production, principally of combines, cartels, and trusts . . . Labour law to be standardised, the right of combination secured . . . The consolidation and extension of income, wealth, and inheritance taxes and their adjustment to the alterations of value and to the efficiency of working capital . . . The safeguarding of the democratic republic . . . All citizens to have right of access to the nation's cultural wealth . . . The international union of the working class on a democratic basis as the best guarantee of peace . . . The revision of the Versailles peace treaty in the direction of economic alleviation and the recognition of rights of national existence.

Part of the Programme of the Social Democratic Party of Germany, decided at Görlitz, 18-24 September 1921

Questions

1 a Using your own knowledge, explain the circumstances in which Source A was issued in November 1918. **(4 marks)**
   b What concerns are identified in Source A? **(6 marks)**
   c How accurate were Liebknecht's concerns? **(5 marks)**

2 a Explain the reference to 'Spartacus, the German Bolsheviks' (line 9 page 41) in Source B. **(3 marks)**
   b What methods are used by the Social Democrats to convey their opposition to Communism (Source B)? **(6 marks)**

3 Using your own knowledge, assess the accuracy of Wolff's interpretation of the political situation in Germany in the early years of the Weimar Republic (Source C). **(6 marks)**

4 Compare and contrast the Spartacist Programme (Source E) with that of the SPD (Source I). **(8 marks)**

5 Using your own knowledge, explain the circumstances in which Noske's Declaration (Source E) was issued. **(4 marks)**

6 a What message is conveyed by the two cartoons in Source F? **(4 marks)**

b How useful are these cartoons as evidence of this period in German history? **(4 marks)**

7 a Using your own knowledge, explain the circumstances in which Kapp's Declaration (Source G) was issued. **(4 marks)**

b Summarise the message of Source G. **(5 marks)**

8 Study Source H. What conclusions may be drawn about:

a The base of support of the Parties shown, in the early years of the Weimar Republic. **(6 marks)**

b The changes there had been in this support since the pre-war period? **(5 marks)**

9 What other information would you need besides Source H to assess the strengths and weaknesses of the political Parties in Germany in the early years of the Weimar Republic? **(6 marks)**

10 'The foundations of the improvised democracy were shaky from the outset.' Use your own knowledge, and Sources A-I, to assess the validity of this interpretation of the early years of the Weimar Republic. **(12 marks)**

6 THE EMERGENCE OF THE NAZI PARTY

The Nazi Party emerged in 1919, but only as one of a number of Right-wing groups mushrooming in Germany. The ideas and slogans it espoused were hardly original. Was it therefore a combination of circumstances and good fortune that eventually resulted in the Nazis emerging head and shoulders above the other movements? How important was Hitler's own dynamic contribution? Clearly his genius for propaganda and speech-making was a bonus, particularly at a time, post-war, and in a place, Bavaria, where politics took on a rabble-rousing, highly-charged character.

The initial smallness of the Nazi movement gave advantages to an energetic, determined leader with self-belief, particularly one able to identify himself with the dissatisfied Bavarians whom he was addressing. Through his personality and local circumstances Hitler was able to achieve dominance within the Party. Features of the movement like the para-military SA, the willingness to employ violence, and the readiness to draft a programme appealing to different interest groups, were not original, but were developed to a fine art by the Nazis. Hitler was even able to exploit an apparent failure like the Munich Putsch of 1923 to his advantage.

Why did the Nazi movement flourish initially in Bavaria, when in the early 1930s the Nazis were to win proportionally more votes in the North German Plain? Why did the Nazis make the particular promises they did in 1920? How significant was the Nazi Programme in gaining support? What type of person became a Nazi in these early years – these 'old fighters' who were to dominate the leadership? Why was such a 'revolutionary' group able to organise and operate with relative freedom? Could the Nazi movement have developed at all but for the peculiar cirumstances prevailing in the early years of Weimar Germany? All these are significant questions when considering the early days of the movement.

A An Early Statement by Hitler
. . . Anti-semitism as a political movement must not be, cannot be, determined by emotional criteria, but only through the recognition of facts. The facts are as follows: First, the Jews are definitely a race and not a religious community . . . a Jew who happens to live among us and is thereby compelled to use the German language cannot be called a German . . . there is living amongst us a non-German, foreign race,

47

unwilling and unable to sacrifice its racial characteristics, to deny its own feeling, thinking and striving, and which none the less possesses all the political rights that we ourselves have. The feelings of the Jews are concerned with purely material things; his thoughts and desires even more so . . . Everything which makes men strive for higher things, whether religion, socialism, or democracy, is for him only a means to an end, to the satisfaction of a lust for money and domination. His activities produce a racial tuberculosis among nations . . .

. . . Anti-semitism based on reason must lead to the systematic legal combating and removal of the rights of the Jew . . . Its final aim, however, must be the uncompromising removal of the Jews altogether. Both are possible only under a government of national strength, never under a government of national impotence.

The Republic in Germany owes its birth not to the united national will of our people but to the cunning exploitation of a series of circumstances which combined to produce a deep general discontent . . . And a large section of our people is aware that no mere change in the form of the State as such can alter or improve our position, but only the rebirth of the moral and spiritual energies of the nation.

This rebirth will be set in motion not by the political leadership of irresponsible majorities under the influence of party dogmas or of an irresponsible press, not by catchwords and slogans of international coinage, but only through the ruthless action of personalities with a capacity for national leadership and an inner sense of responsibility.

From a Statement written by Hitler on 16 September 1919

B An Early Speech by Hitler

. . . Now Hitler turned to deal with the Right and the Left. The nationalists on the Right lack a social sense, the Socialists on the Left a nationalist one. He appeals to the parties on the Right: if you want to be nationalist then come down among your people and put away all your class pride. To the Left he appeals: You who proclaim your solidarity with the whole world, first show your solidarity with your own compatriots, be Germans first and foremost. Do they look like heroes who want to smash the world and yet crawl before foreigners for fear they might not like something they see here? (*applause*) You who are real revolutionaries, come over to us and fight with us for our whole nation (*loud applause*). Your place is not over there with the procurers of international capital, but with us, with your own people!! (*stormy applause*).

Then Hitler turned to the future of Germany, to the youth of Germany, and, in particular, with warm words for their intellectual leaders, the German students. Your place is with us, with the people. You who are still young and still have the fire of enthusiasm in your veins, come over to us, join our fighting party, which pursues its aims ruthlessly, with every means, even with force! (*loud applause*) We are not a class party, but the party of honest producers. Our strength does not lie in the International but in our own strength, that is to say in our people! (*long and stormy applause*)

Notes on a Speech made in Munich on 26 October 1920 (recorded by a member of the Bavarian political police)

C Hitler's Ideas on the NSDAP
The new movement aimed at providing what the others did not: a racialist movement with a firm social base, a hold over the broad masses, welded together in an iron-hard organisation, instilled with blind obedience and inspired by a brutal will, a party of struggle and action . . . If this new kind of movement is to become great and important, its aims must be propagated with fanatical ardour and the total energy of its few supporters must be placed at the service of its propaganda as there is nothing there yet to organise.

Memorandum by Hitler, 7 January 1922

D Another Hitler Speech
. . . There are only two possibilities in Germany: do not imagine that the people will for ever go with the middle party, the party of compromises: one day it will turn to those who have most consistently foretold the coming ruin and have sought to dissociate themselves from it, and that party is either the Left: and then God help us! For it will lead us to complete destruction – to Bolshevism; or else it is a party of despair, when it has lost all its spirit and has no longer any faith in anything, is determined for its part ruthlessly to seize the reins of power – that is the beginning of resistance . . . Here, too, there can be no compromise . . . and there are only two possibilities: either victory of the Aryan or annihilation of the Aryan and the victory of the Jew.

Speech by Hitler, 12 April 1922

E Early Nazi Propaganda
THE ANTI-SEMITES WANT TO
INCITE YOU

Workers, Citizens, Soldiers, Women!

SUPPORT US!
for:
Who are the big capitalists à la Rothschild, Bleichröder,Schwabach?
We Jews!

Who has a greater annual income than Krupp's fortune? A Jew!
Who made the revolution, paid for it, and now wants the rewards?
  We Jews!
Who led and paid the Spartacists and the Bolsheviks? We Jews!
Who alone is 'international', yet is a united race amongst a divided and
incited people? We Jews!
Who offers you truly licentious art in the cinema, cabaret and theatre,
and wants Christian morality to go to the devil? We Jews!
Who sees to it that you can buy on the black market all those goods
which are supposed to be 'unavailable'? We Jews!
Who destroys all bonds of honour, family, nation and society?
  We Jews!
Who frees you from large familes, just so that our own brood can
develop nicely? We Jews!
Who pushes taxes high, so that the banks need not go short? We Jews!

Who frees you from ridiculous German honour, art and customs?
Who roots out both protestantism and catholicism?
Who protects instead
his own Mosaic religion and secret Talmud teachings?

WE JEWS!

So join one of our Jewish controlled political parties.
We Jews Are Your Masters!

We will soon suppress the couple of Germans who want to protect you –
the swastika-louts and the völkisch rabble-rousers.
We'll suppress them just like you.

We'll do it again with your help, dear workers!
Workers, you must be proud to be our slaves and our servants!
We'll pay for everything. You needn't do anything else,
We'll feed you for the rest of your life.

So workers, be our bodyguards! True until death! We have had to
withdraw all our capital for your benefit, so that we are now quite poor.

Help us Dear Worker! Cause a riot in every opponent's meeting! Rip any
leaflet up, unread, that tries to open your eyes. You May Not Read It!

Make the Nazis despicable, by calling them Anti-Semitic
Rowdies, then the German bourgeoisie will fall into line.

Printed Munich. A member of the Jewish race.

A Nazi Leaflet from 1922

Questions

1 Using your own knowledge, state the main themes of the Nazi Programme as first outlined in 1920. **(6 marks)**

2 Compare and contrast the propaganda contained in Sources A-E in terms of content and tone. **(12 marks)**

3 According to Source C, what was to be new about the Nazi movement? **(4 marks)**

4 Using your own knowledge, assess the extent to which the material contained in Sources A-E was typical of Nazi propaganda during the Weimar Republic. **(8 marks)**

7 INFLATION AND PUTSCH:
THE CRISIS OF 1923

1923 might be regarded as the end of the first period of instability and crisis experienced by the Weimar Republic. The year was marked by an economic collapse and the emergence of Hitler on to the national scene.

The economic crisis of 1923 was not caused simply by the huge reparations demands inflicted upon Germany. Inflation had been undermining the economy since 1914, when the Government began to issue war bonds and print money. How much responsibility should German Governments take for the economic difficulties of these years? Wherever responsibility lay, the value of the German mark, already in serious decline, collapsed following the French and Belgian occupation of the Ruhr in 1923, and the policy of 'passive resistance'. How much damage was done by this crisis? Certain groups and individuals benefited: speculators, landholders, many industrialists. Also, the introduction of the *Rentenmark* and the implementation of the Dawes Plan appeared to offer stability again. However, the middle classes (*Mittelstand*) in particular lost out in the process and moved politically towards the Right. The situation of small farmers, weighed down by debt, also worsened. Trade unions lost influence and power. To what extent did the crisis further divide German society? Whilst the economy, aided by foreign money flowing into Germany, recovered, the psychological damage was done. Hyperinflation and the Weimar Republic became almost synonymous in many people's minds. A Government and society already faced with pressing problems found it difficult to live down the memory, particularly when a new economic crisis hit Germany in 1929. Therefore, how significant was 1923 in the ultimate collapse of the Weimar Republic?

Hitler saw the difficulties of 1923 as an opportunity to bring down the Government. A seizure of power in Bavaria, long a hotbed of Communist activity, could coincide with a Right-wing coup in North Germany and hopefully a rising by Right-wing elements within the Army to achieve this goal.

In the event, the Army leaders proved hesitant and the Stresemann Government asserted its authority. Nevertheless, a disappointed Hitler went ahead with his own putsch. Did this experience cause or add to Hitler's distrust of the Army and other 'allies'?

Hitler's isolation ensured the failure of the Beer-Hall Putsch. Hitler's imprisonment (his mild sentence was an indication in itself that his aims had sympathy in some influential quarters) broke the Nazi movement into factions. But the Munich Putsch was important to Hitler's political development. Apart from giving him the opportunity to reflect in prison and dictate *Mein Kampf*, he decided that the way ahead lay not in armed uprising but the creation of a mass political party across Germany. The political system Hitler despised would be used ultimately against itself. The Army command, although nationalist by temperament, could not be trusted. The Nazi Party must become 'respectable' and genuinely national. 1923 was a watershed for Hitler and Germany.

What does 1923 tell us about the development of Hitler's personality? Does it suggest anything about his importance to the Nazi Party? Does 1923 tell us anything about the inherent strengths or weaknesses of the Nazi Party?

A The German Inflation

Economic and social historians are agreed in their view that the widespread belief as to the 'destruction of the middle class' by the inflation is untrue. The 'middle class' consisted of very different groups which were affected in very different ways by the almost complete devaluation of the currency and consequent wiping out of all debts, including those incurred by public bodies. While savers, mortgagees and bondholders lost their wealth and the rentier class disappeared entirely, small tradesmen, shopkeepers and craftsmen did good business and suffered scarcely at all from the inflation, and farmers were on the whole unaffected.

It cannot be denied, however, that the redistribution of wealth within the middle class hastened the dissolution of the German bourgeoisie as a social and political factor; it accentuated the conflicts of wealth within the bourgeois parties and had a lasting effect on the configuration of the party system.

There is disagreement as to the effect of the inflation on real wages and salaries. Until recently, both Marxist and non-Marxist historians have generally believed that the impoverishment of the working class which began during the war continued in 1919-23. This, however, is now being called in question: it is suggested that the level of real wages did not fall steadily during the inflation, but that after 1918-19 the workers' standard of living improved measurably in certain important areas . . .

. . . We know far too little about social divisions among the population, changes in the occupational structure, the extent and nature of women's work, the effects of rationalisation on the labour market, urbanisation and the flight from the land, the falling birth-rate, age structure and urban population . . .

It is generally accepted that the economic situation in Germany was highly precarious even before the world depression . . . the German recession began well before the end of 1929; it was aggravated, but not caused, by the New York stock exchange failure; in this sense we may speak of a 'crisis before the crisis'.

E. Kolb *The Weimar Republic* (English ed. Unwin Hyman 1988)

B Hitler's Justification for the 1923 Putsch

From the very first I have aimed at something more than becoming a Minister. I have resolved to be the destroyer of Marxism. This I shall achieve and once I've achieved that, I should find the title of 'Minister' ridiculous . . .

What did we want on the evening of 8 November? All these gentlemen wanted a Directory in the Reich. If one has striven for something in the Reich, one cannot condemn it in Bavaria . . . We wanted to create in Germany the precondition which alone will make it possible for the iron grip of our enemies to be removed from us. We wanted to create order in the state, throw out the drones, take up the fight against international stock exchange slavery, against our whole economy being cornered by trusts, against the politicising of the trade unions, and above all, for the highest honourable duty which we, as Germans, know should be once more introduced – the duty of bearing arms, military service. And now I ask you: is what we wanted high treason? . . .

The army which we have formed grows from day to day; it grows more rapidly from hour to hour. Even now I have the proud hope that one day the hour will come when these untrained bands will grow to battalions, the battalions to regiments and the regiments to divisions, when the old cockade will be raised from the mire, when the old banners will once again wave before us; and the reconciliation will come in that eternal last Court of Judgement, the Court of God, before which we are ready to take our stand. Then from our bones, from our graves, will sound the voice of that tribunal which alone has the right to sit in judgement upon us. For, gentlemen, it is not you who pronounce judgement upon us, it is the Eternal Court of History which will make its pronouncement upon the charge which is brought against us. The verdict that you will pass I know. But that Court will not ask of us, 'Did you commit high treason or did you not?' That Court will judge us . . . as Germans who wanted the best for their people and their fatherland, who wished to fight and to die. You may pronounce us guilty a thousand times, but the Goddess who presides over the Eternal Court of History will with a smile tear in pieces the charge of the Public Prosecutor and the verdict of this court. For she acquits us.

Hitler's Speech at his Trial for Treason in Munich, February 1924

C Hitler Draws Lessons From the Putsch

. . . When I resume active work it will be necessary to pursue a new policy. Instead of working to achieve power by armed conspiracy, we shall have to hold our noses and enter the Reichstag against the Catholic and Marxist deputies. If outvoting them takes longer than outshooting them, at least the results will be guaranteed by their own Constitution! Any lawful process is slow . . . Sooner or later we shall have a majority and after that we shall have Germany. I am convinced that this is our best line of action now that conditions in the country have changed so radically.

Comments by Hitler in prison in 1924, recorded in K. Ludecke *I Knew Hitler* (London 1938)

D The Aftermath of the Putsch

(i) Hitler rides triumphantly into Berlin with President Ebert in chains

Der Hitler-Prozeß
oder
Wie Kahr das Vaterland gerettet hat

(ii) Erich Schilling in *Simplicissimus*, 17 March 1924. Hitler, on the
shoulders of General Von Lossow, one of the 1923 plotters, tries to
set fire to a building, whilst a swastika comet hurtles across the sky.

Questions

1 What problems of interpreting the economic and social significance of 1923 are suggested by Source A? **(7 marks)**

2 Study Source B:
a How does Hitler justify his actions in attempting the Putsch? **(6 marks)**
b What does this Source reveal about Hitler's style and skills as a political leader and propagandist? **(6 marks)**

3 What, according to Source C, did Hitler learn from the Putsch? **(4 marks)**

4 a What impression of Hitler and the Nazi movement at the time of the 1923 Putsch and its aftermath is suggested by the cartoons in Source D? **(6 marks)**
b How useful and reliable are these cartoons as historical evidence about the impact of Nazism in the early years of the Weimar Republic? **(7 marks)**

8 THE FOREIGN POLICY OF
THE WEIMAR REPUBLIC

The Governments of the early years of the Weimar Republic had little room for manouevre in foreign policy. They were forced to comply with Allied peace terms, however bitter this was for most Germans and whatever the quarrels this engendered amongst politicians.

However, the Weimar Republic soon adopted an independent line in its foreign policy. Notable was the rapprochement with Soviet Russia, formalised in the Treaty of Rapallo of 1922. Was this simply an act of mutual self-interest by two defeated Powers, or part of a traditional German policy of extending influence in Central and Eastern Europe?

Weimar foreign policy is usually identified most closely with Gustav Stresemann, Foreign Minister from 1924 to 1929. His name is linked with the rapprochement with France, formalised in the Treaty of Locarno and German entry into the League of Nations. Yet what were Stresemann's motives? He certainly wished to revise the Treaty of Versailles, particularly its provisions for Germany's Eastern frontiers. Was Stresemann being pragmatic or devious? His politics found more favour with contemporaries abroad and some later historians than with nationalists at home, who accused Stresemann of selling German honour short. Does Stresemann deserve his reputation as a statesman? Would his reputation have been different had he not died in 1929? Could Germany ever hope to regain what Germans regarded as their rightful place in Europe without causing conflict with fearful neighbours? Was the problem of Germany simply, as A. J. P. Taylor asserted, that there was too much of it?

A Stresemann During The First World War

We see the guarantee of a durable peace only in a strong, invulnerable Germany, in security towards East and West. If Belgium is not to become an advanced fort for the enemy again, German military, political and economic supremacy in that country must be secured. At sea Germany must be the ruling power . . . We will not give up the struggle for the world market. On the contrary. Together with our Allies we must create a Central Europe that should be economically and politically of the greatest importance.

Stresemann, speaking in the Reichstag as a National Liberal, 6 April 1916

B Military Perspectives On Foreign Policy

(i) Poland's existence is intolerable, incompatible with the survival of

Germany. It must disappear, and it will disappear through its own internal weakness and through Russia . . With Poland falls one of the strongest pillars of the Treaty of Versailles, the preponderance of France . . . The re-establishment of the broad common frontier between Russia and Germany is the precondition for the regaining of strength of both countries . . .

We aim at two things: first, a strengthening of Russia in the economic and political, thus also in the military field, and so indirectly a strengthening of ourselves, by strengthening a possible ally of the future; we further desire, at first cautiously and experimentally, a direct strengthening of ourselves, by helping to create in Russia an armaments industry which in case of need will serve us . . .

In all these enterprises, which to a large extent are only beginning, the participation and even the official knowledge of the German Government must be entirely excluded.

Memorandum by Seeckt, Head of the Reichswehr, 11 September 1922

(ii) The immediate aim of German foreign policy must be the regaining of full sovereignty over the area retained by Germany, the firm acquisition of those areas at present separated from her, and the re-acquisition of those areas essential to the German economy . . .

These immediate political aims will produce conflict primarily with France and Belgium and with Poland which is dependent on them, then with Czechoslovakia and finally also with Italy . . . It is certainly to be assumed that a reborn Germany will eventually come into conflict with the American-English powers in the struggle for raw materials and markets . . .

Memorandum sent to the German Foreign Office by Stülpnagel, Chief of the Operations Section of the High Command, and approved by Seeckt, 6 March 1926

C Stresemann's Aims In 1925
In my opinion there are three great tasks that confront German foreign policy in the more immediate future –

In the first place the solution of the Reparations question in a sense tolerable for Germany . . .

Secondly, the protection of Germans abroad, those 10 to 12 million of our kindred who now live under a foreign yoke in foreign lands.

The third great task is the readjustment of our eastern frontiers; the recovery of Danzig, the Polish corridor, and a correction of the frontier in Upper Silesia.

In the background stands the union with German Austria, although I am quite clear that this not merely brings no advantages to Germany, but seriously complicates the problem of the German Reich . . . (The

Locarno Pact) rules out the possibility of any military conflict with France for the recovery of Alsace-Lorraine . . .

The question of a choice between east and west does not arise as the result of our joining the League. Such a choice can only be made when backed by military force. That, alas, we do not possess . . .

Letter from Stresemann to the ex-Crown Prince, 7 September 1925

D Interpretations of Stresemann

(i) On the one hand he tried, successfully, to win back international confidence in the peaceful intentions of his policy, while on the other he had to give as much support as he dared to the Reichswehr's efforts at secretly breaking the military restrictions of Versailles. If this policy was two-faced, that was not entirely Stresemann's fault. Without such support, and without such occasional triumphs as the termination of Allied military control or the evacuation of the Rhineland, his efforts at the political and economic rehabilitation of Germany would have foundered on the opposition of the right . . . To go further, however, and say that he was fundamentally opposed to such rearmament would be wrong.

H. W. Gatzke *Stresemann and the Rearmament of Germany* (Norton Library 1969)

(ii) Stresemann's long-term policy was one of preparing for warlike expansion . . . He worked towards a war, but always kept in view that armed force as a political instrument was, under certain conditions, not calculated to serve the interests of the classes he represented.

W. Ruge *Stresemann* (East Berlin 1965)

(iii) Where other Germans insited that revision of the treaty was necessary for the revival of German power, Stresemann believed that the revival of German power would inevitably lead to revision of the treaty . . . But, like Bismarck, he believed that peace was in Germany's interest; and this belief entitles him to rank with Bismarck as a great German, even as a great European, statesman. Maybe even as a greater. His task was certainly more difficult. For Bismarck had only to maintain an existing settlement; Stresemann had to work towards a new one. It is a measure of his success that, while he lived, Europe moved towards peace and treaty revision at the same time.

A. J. P. Taylor *The Origins of the Second World War* (Penguin ed. 1964)

E Weimar Foreign Policy Post-Stresemann

The methods, aims and priorities of Brüning's foreign policy were distinctly different from Stresemann's, involving an aggressive bid for the early solution of the reparation and armament questions. It would probably be too much to interpret this as a clear and irrevocable departure from Stresemann's policy, but certainly 1930 marked 'the switch to a policy of national self-centredness and itensified revisionist claims'. It was also largely owing to the 'radicalisation of international affairs' from 1930/1 onwards that German complaints about the Treaty of Versailles and demands for its revision became louder and shriller with the transition from Stresemann to Brüning and from the latter to the Papen and Schleicher governments.

E. Kolb *The Weimar Republic* (English ed. Unwin Hyman 1988)

Questions

1 Compare and contrast Sources A, B and C in their perception of what should be the aims of German foreign policy. **(8 marks)**

2 To what extent were the foreign policy aims outlined in Sources A, B and C consistent with those proclaimed in Germany before and during the First World War? **(7 marks)**

3 What territories were being referred to in the first paragraph of Source B (ii)? **(4 marks)**

4 To what extent were the tasks outlined by Stresemann in Source C fulfilled during the years of the Weimar Republic? **(6 marks)**

5 a Compare and contrast the interpretations of Stresemann in Source D (i), (ii) and (iii). **(8 marks)**
b To what extent are the claims about Stresemann made in Source D (i), (ii) and (iii) supported by the evidence of Sources A and C? **(8 marks)**

6 Using your own knowledge, assess the validity of the claims made in Source E that Weimar foreign policy changed significantly after Stresemann's death. **(6 marks)**

9 WEIMAR CULTURE

Imperial Germany had not been notable for cultural innovation. However, defeat and a crisis of confidence can break down old barriers and inhibitions, and Weimar Germany became a centre of cultural experimentation, not just for Germany but for Europe's avant garde. German theatre (for example Brecht) and German film (for example Fritz Lang) were highly innovative. Scientists, and the architects of the Bauhaus, achieved world renown. Hermann Hesse and Stefan George were just two members of a galaxy of literary talent. Nor was it just Berlin that witnessed a cultural renaissance: dozens of German towns gave enthusiastic support to the arts. The author Thomas Mann was able to claim with some justice that the 1920s witnessed the shift of Europe's cultural centre from France to Germany.

Germany could be an exciting place to be in the 1920s. Yet, ironically, it was this cultural effervescence which attracted bitter criticism of the Republic from Right-wing political movements like Nazism. Weimar intellectuals were frequently in sympathy with the Left; movements like Modernism were condemned for being out of touch with reality and the experience of the German people – and it is true that there were millions of Germans who were untouched by these developments. Worst still, in the eyes of the Right, trends such as greater freedom for women (expressed in dress and social habits) were associated with Jewish and Bolshevik influences from Soviet Russia. Therefore the Left was unpatriotic, un-German and subversive. These sentiments were ironic, since many Left-wing intellectuals themselves despised the Republic because it tolerated the survival of pre-War institutions.

Cultural liberalism was already on the wane in the years 1930-33. Some intellectuals had already left Germany before the Nazi takeover. The Nazis were to face little overt opposition in their attempts to dismantle Weimar culture. Was this because that culture was as experimental as Weimar democracy, without deep roots, and was never truly representative of the German nation or German spirit as Hitler claimed? Does 'cultural history' matter?

A George Grosz Caricature

Pillars of Society, 1926. Types are represented by a beerglass, a pince-nez, a stand-up collar, a black, white and red flag, a palm leaf, a blood-stained sword. The red nose, the walrus moustache, the duelling scar also characterise leading figures of the Weimar Republic. (See also cover illustration.)

B Otto Griebel

The Internationale, 1929. An example of politically motivated realism. Expressed here is the concept of solidarity.

C John Heartfield

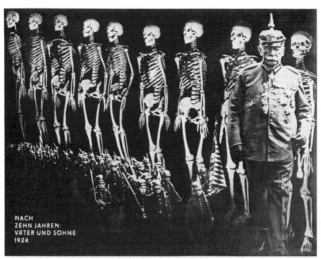

After Ten Years: Fathers and Sons, 1924. Hindenburg appears with the skeletons of those he sent to their deaths in 1914. An example of Heartfield's technique of photomontage, editing several photographs together.

D Heinrich Hoerle

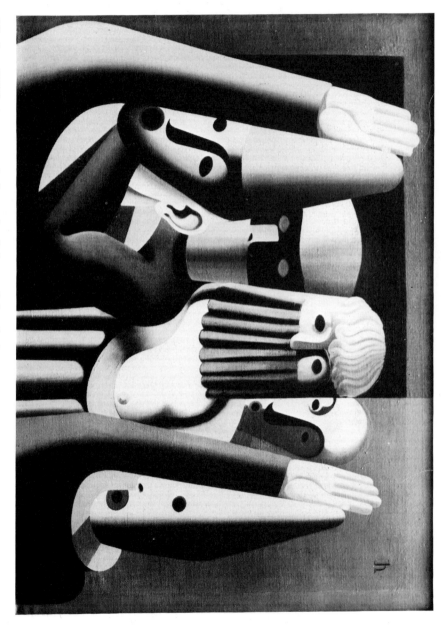

Masken, 1922. An example from the Cologne School of Constructivism. The human form is constructed from geometrically elementary shapes.

E Designs influenced by the Bauhaus

(i) Herbert's Bayer's Design for a Cigarette Kiosk. The cigarette-shaped chimney was to puff smoke rings.

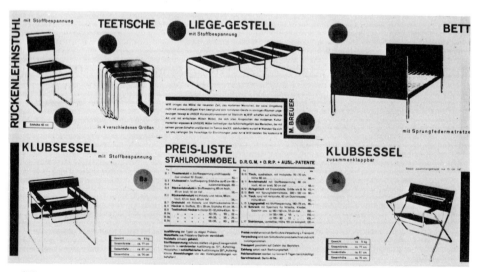

(ii) An Advertising Brochure for Marcel Breuer's 'Standard' mass-produced metal and canvas furniture.

F An Interpretation of Culture

There really was such a phenomenon as 'Weimar culture'; but the term needs to be defined more closely and restrictively, in two respects.

In the first place, the cultural and political life of Weimar Germany were to an unusual extent independent and irrelevant to each other. The liveliness and creativity of the cultural scene did little to win respect for the republic as a political system or to stabilise it as a democracy . . . Many representatives of 'Weimar culture' were caustically critical of specific institutions and were far from identifying with the republic as such . . .

Secondly, the culture of the Weimar period was not confined to the artistic *avant-garde* and the development of a mass culture. The names, titles and achievements associated with the terms 'Weimar culture' and 'golden twenties' are not fully representative of the cultural and intellectual life of the time. 'Modernity' was not the only factor on the cultural scene; the new art was by no means universally popular and accepted, traditional directions and forms were still influential, and modernism was opposed by strong trends of pessimism and anti-modernism. Thus German culture at the time of the Weimar Republic was a deeply divided culture . . . this prevalence of modern trends in literature, painting, architecture and stagecraft, along with manifestations of a freer attitude towards morals and life-style, was fiercely combated by strong conservative, anti-modernist forces that were rooted in broad sections of the population. Their hour was to come in 1933.

E. Kolb *The Weimar Republic* (English ed. Unwin Hyman 1988)

Questions

1 **a** Comment upon the content and style of Sources A-E. **(12 marks)**
  b Which of Sources A-E would be of most use to an historian, and why? **(6 marks)**

2 **a** According to Source F, what problems are there in assessing the importance of cultural developments in the Weimar Republic? **(5 marks)**

  b How would an historian go about assessing the impact of particular cultural developments? **(5 marks)**

3 'Unlimited experimentation and an explosion of novelty.' Using Sources A-F, and your own knowledge, assess the validity of this judgement on the culture of the Weimar Republic. **(10 marks)**

10 IDEOLOGY AND
PROPAGANDA

The Nazi movement in its early years exhibited several characteristics novel in political parties: a paramilitary wing, uniforms, military-style leadership, open resort to violence. However, like other parties, it appeared to have a set of beliefs, or ideology. Nazi ideology can be traced back to several roots: Social Darwinism, a belief in the struggle for survival, translated into race terms; anti-capitalist longings arising from an idealised perception of pre-industrial society; frustrations born out of the experience of war and defeat; and a fervent nationalism, fuelled, not dampened, by the experiences of 1918.

The mish-mash of ideas was expressed in various forms: the 1920 Party Programme; Hitler's speeches and writings; the pseudo-scientific works of 'philosophers' like Rosenberg; and the cruder anti-semitic outpourings of Nazi functionaries like Streicher. It is difficult to establish a coherent Nazi ideology: Hitler forbade discussion of the actual programme after 1926, yet adapted his message to the particular audience to which he was appealing at any given moment. After 1928 Nazi propaganda was geared more and more to the perceived interests of the middle class and rural population, despite the wishes of the more socialist-inclined members of the Party. It is an interesting question as to how far Hitler himself believed in anything strongly other than an obsession with struggle and power.

Ideology had to be translated into propaganda. Some of the most interesting and revealing passages of *Mein Kampf* concern the nature and role of propaganda. Under the influence of Goebbels, in charge of the new Reich Propaganda Department (1930), Nazi propaganda became more sophisticated and systematic. The written word, speeches and posters were supplemented by radio and film.

It is difficult to evaluate precisely the effectiveness of propaganda in influencing opinion, but it is highly likely that Nazi propaganda did play a significant role in attracting membership and votes. Various questions come to mind: was Nazi ideology effectively translated into propaganda? Was Nazi propaganda different and more effective than that of other movements? What characterised Nazi propaganda? Was the nature and function of Nazi propaganda different before and after 1933?

A A Nazi Manifesto
The victory of the nationalist socialist movement will mean the overcoming of the old class and caste spirit. It will allow a nation once more to rise up out of status mania and class madness.

It will train this nation to have an iron determination. It will overcome democracy and reassert the authority of personality.

It will restore justice to the German people through the brutal assertion of the principle that one has no right to hang the little ones so long as the biggest criminals go unpunished and untouched . . .

. . . National Socialism fights for the German worker by getting him out of the hands of his swindlers and destroying the protectors of international bank and stock exchange capital . . .

With its victory the national socialist movement will also seek to guarantee the economic protection of the German people. As long as stock exchanges and department stores are inadequately taxed any further tax increases on the little man are a crime.

With its victory the national socialist movement will protect the peasant through the ruthless education of our people to consume our own products . . .

We will emphasise our national honour and national pride by avoiding all that is foreign as far as possible and giving preference to the results of our own hard work.

We will ensure that the reform of our attitude to defence and a change in our foreign policy will be at the top of the list of reforms . . .

Nazi Party Manifesto issued 10 September 1930

B Nazi Election Propaganda

(i)

'THE GERMAN PEOPLE HAVE WON ALL ALONG THE LINE'

lied the heroes of November 1918 . . .
cried the 'Frankfurter Zeitung', central organ of the

INTERNATIONAL FINANCE-HYENAS

The German people have had ten years to find out just how this victory looks in reality.

WHERE IS THE INTERNATIONAL WORLD REVOLUTION?

It's overdue! The revolution just managed to chisel off the royal insignia from the facade of the post-office, and then it was finished. The storm of the red battalions was spent. It cost a couple of broken windows and a few dead Volkscomrades.

THAT WAS THE REVOLUTION OF THE
SOCIAL DEMOCRACY!

THE RED BOSSES
THE BLACK TOP-HATTERS
and THE GOLDEN DEMOCRATS

have together, delivered our people, sold out and defenceless,

INTO THE HANDS OF INTERNATIONAL WORLD CAPITAL.

'The German army is invincible, but I trust in the German Social
Democrats': so said the Englishman Lloyd George.

I love the German Social Democrats because I wish

THE PEST ON GERMANY

So wrote the Frenchman Leon Daudet. Didn't they put their trust in the
right place?

Haven't we seen the pest in Germany during the last ten years? Black
Frenchmen and slimy Polacks in the service of international high
finance, and because of the treason of the 9th November, they have
become the slave-drivers of Germany.

The German worker lies in beauty and honour on the streets! . . .
Hunger, unemployment, misery, feebleness, tax-torture, inflation-
swindles, corruption, bank-scandals, rubber-truncheons, smash and
grab, those are the results of the Revolution.

GERMANY IS WORTH LESS THAN A NIGGER STATE IN THE WORLD.

The eight-hour day you know only from the picture books of the Social
Democrats. And whilst in the midst of our state, the 'bourgeoisie' and
the 'proletariat' smash in each other's skulls, sinking together into the
yoke of slavery.

THE INTERNATIONAL STOCK EXCHANGE JEWS TRIUMPH

over the bodies of the proletariat and the plundered Mittelstand.

Do you want it to go on forever? Then vote for Scheide- and
Strese-men.

Then vote for the capitalist Dawes parties.

But if you want our race to free itself from today's conditions, then join up with the one party which has prophesied for the last eight years that it would come to this. Join up with the party which is the fanatical enemy of today's state, and which is hated most by its founders, from the Jewish newspapers of the world Stock Exchange, the Frankfurter Zeitung, to the Marxist paper famed for its lies, the Berliner Vorwärts.

VOTE FOR LIST 10

National Socialist German Workers Party (Hitler Movement).

A Nazi Party Election Leaflet, 20 April 1928

(ii)   GERMAN FARMER
                       YOU BELONG TO HITLER!
                              WHY!

The German farmer stands in between two great dangers today:

The one danger is the American economic system – Big capitalism!

it means 'world economic crisis'
it means 'eternal interest slavery' . . .
it means that the world is nothing more than a bag of booty for Jewish
    finance in Wall Street, New York and Paris
it enslaves man under the slogans of progress, technology,
    rationalisation, standardisation, etc.
it knows only profit and dividends
it wants to make the world into a giant trust
it puts the machine over man
it annihilates the independent earth-rooted farmer, and its final aim is
    the world dictatorship of Jewry . . .

it achieves this in the political sphere, through parliament and the swindle of democracy. In the economic sphere, through the control of credit, the mortgaging of land, the Stock Exchange and the Market principle . . .

The Farmer's Leagues, the Landvolk and the Bavarian Farmers' League all pay homage to this system.

The other danger is the Marxist economic system of BOLSHEVISM:

71

it knows only the State economy
it knows only one class, the proletariat
it brings in the controlled economy
it doesn't just annihilate the self-sufficient farmer economically – it
    roots him out . . .
it brings the rule of the tractor
it nationalises the land and creates mammoth factory-farms
it uproots and destroys man's soul, making him the powerless tool of
    the communist idea – or kills him
it destroys the family, belief and customs . . .
it is anti-Christ, it desecrates the churches . . .

its final aim is the world-dictatorship of the proletariat, that means
ultimately the world dictatorship of Jewry, for the Jew controls this
powerless proletariat and uses it for his dark plans.

Big Capitalism and Bolshevism work hand in hand; they are born of
Jewish thought and serve the master plan of world Jewry.

Who alone can rescue the farmer from these dangers?

NATIONAL SOCIALISM!

A Nazi Leaflet produced during the Presidential Election Campaign of 1932

(iii)

| GERMAN WOMEN! | GERMAN MOTHERS! |
| GERMAN WOMEN! | GERMAN MOTHERS! |

Our Young People Defiled:

Dr. Zacharias, Dresden, reports as follows:

The present Prussian Welfare Minister Hirtsiefer has confirmed after
questions were asked, that in a German Grammar School for Girls 63
per cent of girls had experienced sexual intercourse and 47 per cent had
some form of sexual disease . . .

The number of sexual offences and cases of incest pile up in the most
gruesome manner! Since January 1st 1932, 92 convictions against sex
offenders have been reported, of which 12 cases were incest, 5 of sexual
murder, 40 offences against children and 35 were offences against
adults.

This is a result of the many years during which our people, and in
particular our youth, have been exposed to a flood of muck and filth, in

word and print, in the theatre and in the cinema. These are the results of the systematic Marxist destruction of the family. And all this despite the fact that we have a chancellor of the 'Christian Centre Party', and despite the fact of a Hindenburg, who as President watches over the constitution, which according to Article 122 is supposed to protect our youth against spiritual, bodily and moral harm.

Is there no possibility of salvation? Must our people, our youth, sink without hope of rescue into the muck and filth? No!!! The National Socialists must win the election so that they can put a halt to this Marxist handiwork, so that once again women are honoured and valued, and so that the cinema and the theatre contributes to the inner rebuilding of the nation.

German women and mothers. Do you want your honour to sink still further?

Do you want your daughters to be playthings and the objects of sexual lust?

If NOT then vote for a National Socialist Majority on JULY 31st.

Then vote for

LIST TWO

HITLER-MOVEMENT   NAT. SOCIAL GERMAN
                                           WORKERS PARTY

Nazi Leaflet issued during the Reichstag Elections, 31 July 1932

C Nazi Propaganda Posters

(i) *Work and Bread*

(ii) *Death to Lies* (Marxism and Big Business)

(iii) *The Last Push*. The Catholic Centre Party and the Communists are crushed.

Questions

1 Using your own knowledge, assess the extent to which the ideology and message of Source A was consistent with the original Nazi programme.

(7 marks)

2 Study Sources A-C:

a Compare and contrast these Sources in terms of their content and style. **(10 marks)**

b Who was the propaganda in these Sources aimed at? **(7 marks)**

3 To what extent does the bias in Sources B and C reduce their value as evidence to the historian? You should refer to the Sources in your answer. **(7 marks)**

4 Using your own knowledge, estimate the importance of propaganda in the rise of the Nazis. **(8 marks)**

11 THE LAST YEARS OF THE WEIMAR REPUBLIC

The Nazi Party scored spectacular successes in the Reichstag elections of September 1930. This continued a trend already in evidence as the Nazis exploited rual discontent in 1928 and the international economic crisis which broke in 1929. All the political parties were forced to consider their positions. For example, the KPD now concentrated their attacks on the SPD or the 'Social Fascists'; and the Centre Party moved to the Right. The Nazis did not alter their Programme, but showed skill in exploiting difficult situations through a combination of propaganda and Hitler's leadership.

Weimar Governments were unable to resolve the crisis. Brüning's attempts to alleviate the situation between 1930-32 were not negligible, but his Government lacked support both nationwise and amongst powerful Conservative forces. Brüning's successors, von Papen and von Schleicher, had powerful Conservative backers but no parliamentary majorities or mass support. Increasingly, Hitler was courted as leader of a mass Party, albeit a leader who might be manipulated. Hitler displayed skill and nerve in refusing to compromise over the Chancellorship, even when his Party's growth in popularity was checked at the polls in November 1932. His reward was to be taken on board by the Conservative Establishment in January 1933. He was then in a position to begin his own revolution.

Several questions may be posed. To what extent was Hitler's success due to his own skill or the machinations of others? Was Hitler brought to power by popular support or intrigue? Why were various groups and individuals – the Left, The President, and the Army for example – unwilling or unable to stop Hitler? Was the Weimar Republic already too exhausted or seen as not worth fighting for? How important were local factors, documented for example in Allen's study of Northeim, in the Nazi success? On a broader level, would the Weimar Republic have survived but for the Great Depression of 1929 – the economy was already recovering when Hitler was appointed Chancellor? Did it simply have too few really committed supporters to survive at all? Did the Nazis only succeed because they were a movement of protest, and knew how to protest effectively? Did January 1933 represent a real revolution, and was it avoidable?

A Problems of the Political System

(i) Oskar Garvens *A Breakdown: A Pleasing Phenomenon!* **1932. The German citizen in the centre of the wheel shows no interest, surrounded by competing political parties.**

(ii) Looked at politically, objectively, the result of the election [Summer 1932] is so fearful because it seems clear that the present election will be the last normal Reichstag election for a long time to come. The so-called race of thinkers and poets is hurrying with flags flying towards dictatorship and thus towards a period that will be filled with severe revolutionary disturbances. The elected Reichstag is totally incapable of functioning, even if the Centre goes in with the National Socialists, which it will do without hesitation if it seems in the interests of the party. Genuine bourgeois parties no longer exist. The bourgeoisie has excluded itself as a factor in the political process and will probably have to pay dearly for it.

The one consolation could be the recognition that the National Socialists have passed their peak, since, in comparison with the Prussian elections, they have declined in most constituencies, but against this stands the fact that the radicalism of the right has unleashed a strong radicalism on the left. The Communists have made gains almost everywhere and thus internal political disturbances have become exceptionally bitter. If things are faced squarely and soberly the situation is such that more than half the German people have declared themselves against the present state, but have not said what sort of state they would accept. Thus any organic development is for the moment impossible. As the lesser of many evils to be feared, I think, would be the open assumption of dictatorship by the present government.

From a Memorandum by Dr. Kulz, Reich Minister of the Interior, 1932

B Political Manouevrings

(i) Through the attempt of the Papen Government to exclude Adolf Hitler from power, we have come into sharp conflict with a certain kind of anti-social and therefore capitalistic concept of economics. This opposition is justified and must be carried out with all our strength.

But it may not lead to a complete condemnation of all employers as such and thereby get into the deep waters of Marxist class war. For instance, it is wrong to equate, as Marxism does, employers with exploiters . . .

It is also wrong to make industry as a whole responsible for the deficiency of the Papen agrarian programme, as has happened now and then . . .

In every political situation we must adhere to the old, tried guidelines of National Socialism; not treating all business alike in the Marxist way, but distinguishing strictly between healthy business leadership, which is indispensable to the economy, and exploiters. To talk of the expropriation of all industrial concerns is, of course, a direct contravention of National Socialist principles.

Moreover, the fight against the Papen Cabinet must not develop into a fight against the aristocracy as such. We must always be aware of the fact that the best part of the German aristocracy fights in our own ranks and therefore does not deserve to be demoted from the German front just because of a few black sheep.

Confidential Memorandum from Nazi Propaganda Organiser Goebbels, October 1932

(ii) Papen was dismissed because he wanted to fight the National Socialists and did not find in the Reichswehr the necessary support for such a policy, and . . . Schleicher came to power because he believed he could form a government which would have the support of the National Socialists. When it became clear that Hitler was not willing to enter Schleicher's Cabinet and that Schleicher on his part was unable to split the National Socialist Party, as he had hoped to do with the help of Gregor Strasser, the policy for which Schleicher had been appointed Chancellor was shipwrecked. Schleicher was aware that Hitler was particularly embittered against him because of his attempt to break up the Party, and would never agree to cooperate with him. So he now changed his mind and decided to fight against the Nazis . . . Schleicher came to Hindenburg therefore with a demand for emergency powers as a prerequisite of action against the Nazis . . . Hindenburg declared that he was unable to give him such a blank cheque and must reserve to himself decisions on every individual case. Schleicher for his part said that under these circumstances he was unable to stay in office and tendered his resignation on 28 January . . . despite Papen's persuasions, Hindenburg was extremely hesitant, until the end of January, to make Hitler Chancellor. He wanted to have Papen again as Chancellor. Papen finally won him over to Hitler with the argument that the representatives of the other right-wing parties which would belong to the Government would restrict Hitler's freedom of action. In addition Papen expressed his misgivings that, if the present opportunity were again missed, a revolt of the National Socialists and civil war were likely.

Account by Otto Meissner, State Secretary in the Reich President's Office, made to the Nuremberg Tribunal after the Second World War

(iii) Karl Holtz cartoon in *Der Wahre Jakob*, 16 July 1932. 'Papen's government has said that it would adapt itself to the poverty of the nation. The process of adapting itself to the intellectual poverty of the nation has already taken place'. Papen and his ministers read Goebbels' propaganda journal, *Der Angriff*; the Nazi newspaper, *Völkischer Beobachter* lies on the table; Hitler's portrait has replaced Hindenburg's; the notice reads 'Imperial Chancellery. Entry only by permission of Herr Regierungsrat Hitler.'

C SPD Attitudes

(i) ... The organisations united in the Iron Front are absolutely convinced that a *unification of the proletariat is more essential than ever before*. The fascist danger demands this unity. The danger of fascism however can only be countered when a *genuine* common will to unity is present ...

But you have made it impossible to pursue the necessary united front against fascism because of your year-long attempts to subvert and dismember strong workers' organisations, your common cause with the fascists both inside and outside parliament, your attempts to cripple the Trade Union movement through the Revolutionary Trade Unions, and your slogans, 'Severing – the same as Hitler' and 'Social Democracy – the real enemy'.

Declaration by the Iron Front (SPD anti-fascist Front) to the KPD (*German Communist Party*) in *Vorwärts*, 18 June 1932

(ii) *The Worker in the Land of the Swastika! Vote Social Democrat List 1*

D Communist Attitudes

(i) *For Bread and Freedom*

(ii) *Solidarity with Soviet Russia*

(iii) *For a Red Workers Saxony*

E Approaching the End

(i) Karl Arnold, *Hitler, The National Marxist* in *Simplicissimus*, 1930.
'Adolf, Adolf, give me some of my theories back.'

S.M. ADOLF

Ich
führe Euch herrlichen Pleiten entgegen!

(ii) John Heartfield *His Majesty Adolf* 24 August 1932. 'I lead you towards magnificent disasters!' (a play on the words of Kaiser Wilhelm II's boast 'I lead you towards a magnificent era.')

ADOLF – DER ÜBERMENSCH

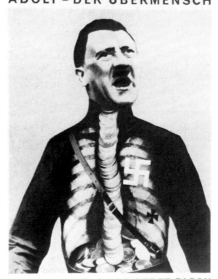

SCHLUCKT GOLD UND REDET BLECH

(iii) John Heartfield *Adolf, the Superman! Swallows Gold and Talks Crap* 17 July 1932

(iv) Paul Weber *Hitler – A German Fate* **1932**

Questions

1 What can you infer from Sources A (i) and (ii) about the state of politics in Germany between 1930 and 1932? **(7 marks)**

2 Using your own knowledge, explain the extent to which the fears of the writer in Source A (ii) were justified by subsequent events. **(6 marks)**

3 a What were Goebbels' concerns, as expressed in Source B (i)? **(4 marks)**

 b To what extent were Goebbels' instructions in Source B (i) consistent with earlier Nazi propaganda? **(6 marks)**

4 a 'Hitler came to power by backstairs intrigue.' To what extent is this assertion justified by Sources B (ii) and (iii)? **(7 marks)**

 b What impression is given of Von Papen and other Weimar politicians by Sources B (ii) and (iii)? **(6 marks)**

5 a Using your own knowledge, explain the background to the SPD complaints in Source C (i). **(3 marks)**

 b What are the uses and limitations of Source C (i) to an historian of this period? **(4 marks)**

6 What were the main SPD concerns as expressed in Source C? **(6 marks)**

7 What were the main Communist concerns as expressed in the posters in Source D? **(4 marks)**

8 Compare and contrast the content and style of the propaganda in Sources C and D with Nazi propaganda of the same period. **(9 marks)**

9 a Compare and contrast the methods by which Hitler and the Nazis were presented in the extracts in Source E. **(7 marks)**

 b Take any two examples from Source E and explain the background or context of the representations shown. **(6 marks)**

10 Use Sources A-E to consider the truth of the argument that, from 1930 onwards, 'democracy in the Weimar Republic had little chance of survival.' **(12 marks)**

12 HISTORIOGRAPHY

The period of German history from 1890 to 1933 has evoked considerable controversy amongst historians, both German and others. Some debate concerns particular incidents; some concerns broader themes – for example, was Nazism an aberration or a logical development in the context of German history? Not at all the issues can be included in this volume, but there are several of interest. They include the controversy kindled by the German historian Fritz Fischer, with his claim that Germany's leaders deliberately engineered war in 1914 in order to pursue expansionist aims. Some historians have addressed the issue of the extent of which Hitler's own aims derived from trends already inherent in German history. There is also a debate about the nature of the Weimar Republic itself. Did it ever possess a real chance? What about the Nazis: how new and radical were they?

For a long time historical research into the Weimar Republic concentrated on the final years, in an attempt to explain its demise. Was the overthrow of the Weimar Republic an 'act of fate', a product of historical circumstances, or the outcome of the actions of manipulative groups and individuals, taking advantage of particular circumstances? Did big business help Hitler to power? How can voting patterns be explained: they were more complex than is sometimes claimed? Was Presidential government after 1930 a disaster?

Later research focussed on the early period of the Weimar Republic. Could the failure of the Weimar democracy be explained by structural defects built into the system, such as an anti-democratic judiciary? Liberal-minded historians wondered why there was never a solid backbone of support for the Republic.

Only in more recent years has there been a systematic study of the intervening years of the Republic, the years often labelled the 'Stresemann era' or the 'years of stability'. Did the Weimar politicians miss the opportunity to consolidate the Republic after 1924? Is the very division into historical 'eras' misleading?

Some interesting research has emerged. For example, it is now evident that fundamental differences between employers and trade unions emerged strongly after 1924, during the period of recovery, culminating in the Ruhr dispute of 1928. This evidence, together with research into the relationship between wages, prices and investment, suggests that the German economy was on a slippery slope well before the Depression 'officially' hit Germany in 1929.

Another area of controversy during this period concerns German foreign policy. To what extent was Stresemann a German nationalist, or a European statesman? Could his revisionist foreign policy have ever succeeded without conflict? Was there continuity in Weimar foreign policy?

All that a study of the historiography of this period shows with certainty is that simplistic assertions and interpretations can be dangerously misleading, and that historical research into pre-Nazi Germany continues to be an area of controversy and interest.

A Continuity and German History

(i) Neither the 'Third Reich' nor the related Second World War would have been possible without the alliance between the former petty-bourgeois Hitler, the rabble-rouser and monomaniac, and the traditional agrarian and industrial power elites who dominated both the armed forces and the diplomatic service. They 'represented the continuity of the national-state legacy' to a particularly high degree: 'They had consciously experienced the rise of Germany prior to 1914, and they were contemporaneous with the economic and military springs of German Great-Power policy in all its variations. Such massive armaments and gearing of the economy to military preparedness would not have been possible without them.' Over and above mere revision of Versailles, their general objective was the rehabilitation of the German Great-Power position, above all with 'regard to eastern Europe, to an eastern imperium guaranteeing a self-sufficient war economy' . . . This objective had originated during the Kaiserreich, led to the First World War, seemed to find realisation in the peace of Brest-Litovsk, lay dormant during the interregnum of the Weimar republic (which continued to call itself the German Empire) and gathered momentum during the Third Reich and into the Second World War . . . On two occasions, during the Kaiserreich and in Hitler's Reich, the dominant elites of the German Empire misunderstood the historical and political realities confronting Germany in the modern world. They failed to recognise (1) that their attempt to evade societal change in the age of industry by asserting their privileged social position at home, and by also resorting in an emergency to military expansion abroad, was doomed to failure. They failed to understand (2) that neither their European neighbours nor the USA would ever willingly accept a German hegemony based on military expansion . . . the catastrophes of German history were not 1918 and 1945, as German tradition prefers to believe, but rather 1914 and 1933/39 . . .

Fritz Fischer *From Kaiserreich To Third Reich* (English ed. Unwin Hyman 1986)

(ii) It would perhaps be more helpful to think in terms of 'continuities' rather than 'continuity' – of a number of traditions which, like the strands of a thick rope, are intertwined but can be separated by careful analysis. There is, for instance, a striking similarity between Stresemann's demand for the restoration of the 1914 eastern frontier and the Anschluss of the Sudentenland, of Austria and the German parts of the South Tyrol on the one hand, and the persistent demand for the same areas by Hitler's conservative opponents after 1938 . . . Hitler's aims in turn bear a striking resemblance to the aims pursued by the Kaiser's Germany in the First World War, and particularly . . . those pursued by Ludendorff in the east in 1918. Here, then, are two powerful but fairly distinct traditions. How far either of them can be followed back beyond the First World War and the collapse of the Austro-Hungarian empire, is a difficult question to answer . . .

In the last analysis, seeing continuity in history means seeing things from a certain distance. To most Germans living through the upheavals of 1918, it seemed as if a world was coming to an end. Only with the wisdom of hindsight can the historian discern that the change was less fundamental than contemporaries supposed, that the thrones fell but the old army, the old bureaucracy, the old university professors, the old party leaders, the old internal boundaries, remained . . . Only from the perspective of the distant observer do Bethmann Hollweg's aims in the First World War seem to coincide largely with those of Ludendorff, who overthrew him, or Stresemann's with those of Seeckt, who came close to so doing.

J. C. G. Röhl *From Bismarck to Hitler* (Longman 1970)

B The Fall Of The Weimar Republic

What made Hitler possible? Was the Nazi 'seizure of power' inevitable in the circumstances that prevailed? . . . Certainly, the monocausal explanations which at first prevailed, attributing the rise of Nazism and Hitler's assumption of power to a single cause or a single main cause, are by now discarded, as all such simplistic accounts have proved inadequate. Historians today at least agree that the collapse of the republic and the Nazi 'seizure of power' can only be plausibly explained in terms of a very complex range of causes. Among these, the following must be taken into account: (1) the institutional framework, for example, the President's constitutional rights and options, especially in the absence of clear parliamentary majorities; (2) economic developments, with their effect on the political and social balance of power; (3) the peculiarities of German political culture (partly responsible, for example, for the disaffection of the elite classes who, for the most part, were hostile to the pluralistic party, democracy of the republic); (4) changes in the social fabric, especially in the 'middle class', with consequences, *inter alia*, for its political orientation and electoral behaviour; (5) ideological factors (the German authoritarian tradition; extreme nationalism, exacerbated by defeat in war, by the 'stab in the back' legend and by propaganda against the 'war guilt' charge; the yearning for a 'strong man', which prepared the way for a charismatic 'leader' cult such as Hitler's); (6) factors of mass psychology, for example, the effect of propaganda enhanced by the rootlessness and political instability of large sections of the population; and (7) the role of certain key personalities, in particular Hindenburg, Schleicher and Papen.

Our answer to the question as to what brought down the Weimar Republic and made Hitler possible will largely be qualified by the weight attached to the different components, and how they are woven into a consistent whole; for this weighting and combining is not dictated by the sources, but is the task of the interpreting historian. How it is performed will depend on shifts of interest and the viewpoint of the individual inquirer or of a whole generation of researchers, determined by their horizon of experience, scale of values and standards of judgement.

E. Kolb *The Weimar Republic* (English ed. Unwin Hyman 1988)

Questions

1 Using Sources A (i) and (ii), and your own knowledge, explain why the issue of 'continuity' has been particularly important in the interpretation of German history between 1890 and 1933.   **(10 marks)**

2 What does Source B suggest about:
   a The reasons for the collapse of the Weimar Republic.   **(6 marks)**
   b The problems of historical interpretation generally?   **(5 marks)**

3 *Either* assess the contribution of any one historian to your understanding of this period; *or* identify any particular problem or issue in German history from this period and examine how it has been approached by historians.   **(12 marks)**

13 DEALING WITH EXAMINATION QUESTIONS

Specimen Source Question Answer

(See page 51)

1 Using your own knowledge, state the main themes of the Nazi Programme as first outlined in 1920. **(6 marks)**

The Nazi Programme of 1920 is often referred to as the 25 Point Programme, since it was divided into 25 paragraphs. These can be grouped into several themes. Firstly, there were a number of Nationalist demands, chiefly concerned with the unification of all Germans in a Greater Germany, equality for Germany in her dealing with other nations, revision of the Peace Treaties, and a demand for more land and colonies in order to feed the German population. There were also several racist demands: only those of German blood were to enjoy protection of the law, immigration was to be controlled, and, specifically, Jews were to be denied citizenship. Finally there were several Socialist or anti-capitalist clauses, for example urging profit-sharing in large industries and the 'communalising' of large department stores. Concern was also expressed to raise health, educational and cultural standards. A strong central government was called for. In short, the Programme contained a number of specific demands calculated presumably to appeal to nationalist and anti-capitalist sentiments in the German population.

2 Compare and contrast the propaganda contained in Sources A-E in terms of content and tone. **(12 marks)**

Source A illustrates two principal themes. Firstly, Hitler gives his rationale for anti-Semitism; secondly, he stresses the need for the 'moral and spiritual' rebirth of Germany. In Source B Hitler appeals to both Right and Left to join the Nazis. Source C returns to the theme of racialism, but also gives some ideas on the organisation of the movement and the methods by which its ideology may be promoted. In Soure D anti-Communism emerges as a theme, together with anti-Semitism again. Source E is permeated throughout with anti-Semitism.

There are similarities and differences between these Sources both in content and tone. Source A purports to be a scientific, factual analysis of the differences between Jews and Germans. Actually there are no hard facts, but Hitler presents his case as a justification for removing the rights of Jews in Germany. At the same time Hitler condemns the structure of the Weimar Republic and calls for a strong Government. The tone is clearly anti-democratic in the sense that party politics are belittled through the use of words like 'dogmas', 'slogans', and 'irresponsible majorities'. 'Ruthless action' is advocated, and there is a direct appeal for 'national leadership', presumably a dictator. The tone is relatively moderate compared to some Nazi propaganda, but it is full of assertions rather than provable facts.

The message of Source B is slightly different. Hitler cleverly appeals to both Left and Right, by stressing the virtues of a classless, truly German, society. The tone is clearly designed to appeal to nationalist sentiment: hence phrases like 'crawl before foreigners'. Hitler also appeals to youth. As in Source A, internationalism is condemned, and the phrase 'ruthless' occurs again.

Source C is perhaps more directly emotional, appealing to 'fanatical ardour' and 'energetic action'. Once again the idea of ruthlessness is conveyed. It occurs also in Source D. In Source D the idea of struggle re-emerges. Compromise is damned: there must be determined action.

Source E is very racist, but the difference between it and the other Source lies in its heavy sarcasm and method of approach. A series of rhetorical, exaggerated questions is asked, all designed to portray the Jews as money-grabbing, deceitful manipulators, running Germany in their own interests. The entire pamphlet is designed to stir up hatred and other strong emotions. In fact the element common to all the Sources is the attempt to arouse emotions and present crude assertion as established fact, whatever the differences between individual Sources.

3 According to Source C, what was to be new about the Nazi movement?

(4 marks)

In Source C Hitler claims that his movement is new basically for this reason: although racialism is not new, a racialist philosophy has never before been propagated by a large, 'brutal', fanatically-supported Party. In short, the Nazi Party is only for fanatics and fighters, prepared to follow their leader, like soldiers in an elite army. This represents a very different style from that of a democratic Party.

4 Using your own knowledge, assess the extent to which the material contained in Sources A-E was typical of Nazi propaganda during the Weimar Republic. **(8 marks)**

The material in Sources A-E is typical of much Nazi propaganda during the Weimar Republic, but there were many types of propaganda. At one extreme there were the crude anti-Semitic outpourings of Streicher's *Der Stürmer*, specialising for example in racist cartoons and stories of Jewish sacrifices of Christian children and other 'race crimes'. This sort of propaganda makes the anti-Semitic message of Source E appear quite subtle. At the other extreme were the pseudo-scientific outpourings of a Nazi theoretician like Rosenberg, who attempted to provide a philosophical justification for Nazi policies not evident in these Sources.

Nazi propaganda was varied, and its nature changed. Some of the cruder racism of these Sources was less in evidence towards the end of the Weimar Republic when Hitler was trying to appeal to a wide cross-section of the electorate and also big business. Some of the extreme propaganda was actually toned down. Careful attention was also paid to regional variations and needs. This was the responsibility of Goebbels, who centralised control of propaganda after 1930. There was an increasing emphasis on rallies and appeals to young people. Certain themes, notably nationalist propaganda, remained consistent. Some propaganda was targeted on specific groups. Therefore some of the propaganda in these Sources is typical, but there were many other examples besides – and providing a rich diet of propaganda was one of the consummate skills of both Hitler and Goebbels.

Approaching Essay Questions

The key to writing successful history essays must always be in the last resort the ability to achieve relevance; in other words, you must answer the particular question set. Relevance is worth much more than length or a mass of detail. Accurate knowledge is also important, but only if it is employed to back up a particular argument, and not for its own sake. Unanalytical narrative, or prepared answers to a topic which do not meet the requirements of the particular title set, are probably the commonest failings of examination answers. Conversely, the best answers are often concise, always relevant, analytical, and show evidence of wide and thoughtful reading. Your command of the English language is not being tested as such, but you must be able to present your arguments effectively!

Plan your essays. Break the question down into its key components. What are the key phrases or words in the question? Give your essays a shape: an introduction which will introduce the main argument and possibly indicate how you hope to approach it; a logical main body, written in paragraphs (sometimes ignored by students!); and a conclusion which does not repeat the bulk of your essay but neatly draws together the threads. Other issues, such as style and use of quotations, are also important if you wish to write lucidly and well. As with most things in life, essay writing usually improves with practice!

In most of the history essays you encounter, you will be asked to evaluate a statement or quotation, or answer a direct question. There are usually different approaches you may adopt: therefore 'model' answers must be treated with caution. It is, for example, quite in order to approach a controversial issue by considering evidence which supports different sides of an argument, without necessarily coming down decisively on one side of a particular interpretation. On the other hand, it is equally acceptable to argue a particular viewpoint, provided you can produce supporting evidence. Credit will usually be given if you show relevant knowledge of contemporary and/or more recent sources.

There are books available which deal in some depth with issues such as analytical reading, question analysis and essay-writing. Students may well find any of the following useful:

C. Brasher: *The Young Historian* (OUP 1970)
J. Cloake, V. Crinnon and S. Harrison: *The Modern History Manual* (Framework Press 1987)
J. Fines: *Studying To Succeed – History at 'A' Level and Beyond* (Longman 1986)

The following list of essay titles on Germany 1890-1933 includes suggestions (no more than suggestions!) on how to approach them; plus a specimen answer. Use them as part of your course or for examination practice.

Possible Essay Titles

1 'Wilhelmine Germany was full of internal contradictions.' Is this an accurate description of Germany between 1890 and 1914?

This question merits careful analysis. Political, economic and social structures should be identified and analysed in order to establish the overall truth or otherwise of the assertion. Political life was complex: you should analyse the Constitution; relations between the Emperor, ministers and the Reichstag; relations between Reichstag and Bundesrat; relations between the states and the federal government. Economically Germany was strong, but industrialisation created its own strains which should be analysed. Socially Germany was divided: there was urbanisation and rapid change, but traditional class structures were slow to break down. An overall assessment of Germany on the eve of the First World War would be helpful.

2 Why and with what consequences did Imperial Germany pursue a policy of *Weltpolitik?*

This is a two-part question. Bülow referred to *Weltpolitik* in 1897. Why did Germany pursue a drive for world power? Various factors to be analysed include the Kaiser's personal ambition; the role of powerful pressure groups; economic and military pressures; and nationalist sentiment. The consequences may be divided into short and long term. In the short term, you should assess the progress of Germany's drive for colonies, and the result of Germany's provocative behaviour in various parts of the world. In the long run it might be argued that the failure of German diplomacy and her assertive behaviour in the early years of this century were major contributory factors in causing the First World War – a very important consequence!

3 'Unfriendly and provocative.' To what extent is this an accurate summary of German policies towards the European Powers between 1890 and 1914?

A sensible approach to this question would be, first of all, to identify what Germany's policies actually were: her relationship with the Great Powers; her imperial policy; and her part in international crises in Morocco and the Balkans. There is plenty of scope for careful analysis: in the case of certain Powers, notably Austria, it is clear that Germany's attitude was fundamentally friendly and supportive (for example in the 1908 Bosnian Crisis); in the case of others, notably France, it might be described as provocative (for example the Moroccan Crises); with some Powers, for example Britain, German policy sometimes seemed provocative (for example the 'naval race'), whereas sometimes there was talk of friendship or even alliance. Given the fact that some elements of German foreign policy are likely to be identified as unfriendly and provocative, some attempt should be made to explain the reasons for this: how much was due to the Kaiser, to his ministers, to his military leaders, to pressure groups, and so on.

4 'To some German leaders, war in 1914 seemed to offer a solution to the growing threats to their country from external and internal forces.' Explain this statement.

There are several strands to this question, and terms of reference should be clearly defined. Firstly, the 'German leaders' should be identified, and the relationship between them: the Kaiser, politicians (notably Bethmann Hollweg) and Army leaders. Then the 'external forces' and 'internal forces' must be identified and analysed. The former may be identified as the perceived threat from the activities of the Triple Entente; the latter would include the perceived threat to internal stability from the growing Socialist movement and the social pressures resulting chiefly from industrialisation. Some discussion of the extent to which those 'German leaders' actually prompted war in 1914 is then called for.

5 What effect did the First World War have on Germany?

This is not an invitation to write about military events, but the question should be addressed in terms of the immediate, short-term and long-term consequences of the War: the economic effects; the effects on German psychology and nationalist sentiment; and on the political and social foundations of society. The long-term consequences are perhaps most difficult to assess. You must consider the shock of defeat; the political, economic and social dislocations caused by the War and their influence on the early years of the Weimar Republic. Indeed, you might argue that

Germans never came to terms with the effects of the War and its aftermath, and that was a reason for the ultimate downfall of the Republic.

6 What was the significance of the German Revolution of 1918?

The obvious answer is that is was very significant. You should discuss the resignation of the Kaiser and the birth of the Weimar Republic. However, you should then consider what (politically, economically, socially) survived 1918 or was adapted. Less concrete aspects such as ideas (nationalism, democracy) should also be considered. Finally you should assess to what extent 1918 was a fundamental revolution *at all* for Germany.

7 To what extent had the Weimar Republic overcome its problems by 1929?

Firstly the problems need identifying. These may be classified as structural (to do with the actual Constitution); political (to what extent were problems brought on by misguided policies); and 'external', that is, problems created by circumstances such as the Peace settlement and the 1923 Crisis with which the Republic had to deal. There is likely to be a distinction between the initial years of crisis after the War, and the so-called 'period of stability' from 1924 to 1929. Reference should also be made to Stresemann and his foreign policy. Beware of assuming a sharp division between these periods. Recent research suggests considerable continuity: for example, the Republic was experiencing economic problems well before 1929. There may be discussion as to whether the Weimar Republic *ever* overcame its problems.

8 Why was the Weimar Republic able to survive the crisis years of 1919-21 but not those of 1929-33?

Clearly the essential feature of your answer should be comparison and contrast. A brief description of the events of these crisis years is necessary; then an analysis of them in context. For the 1919-21 period you should analyse the Left and Right Wing coup attempts and why they failed. For the second period you should discuss the economic crisis and its political implications. By the early 1930s the opposition groups, especially on the Right, were stronger and more organised; possibly disillusionment with the Republic was more pronounced by then. Concentrate on an analytical comparison and contrast rather than narrative.

9 Assess Stresemann's contribution to the Weimar Republic.

The answer is likely to concentrate on Stresemann's foreign policy: the Treaty of Locarno, Germany's entry into the League of Nations, and the rapprochement with Britain and France. You will need to discuss the degree to which these events helped the image of the Republic and aided stability, along with Stresemann's aims. There should be a good opportunity here to consider some of the historiographical interpretations of Stresemann's role in the Republic.

10 'A remarkably fruitful decade in intellectual and artistic matters.' Is this an accurate description of Weimar culture in the 1920s?

To attempt this question a detailed knowledge of all cultural developments is not expected, but you should be able to describe at least some of the principal aspects of culture at this time – literary, artistic, architectural, theatrical and cinematic. A sophisticated answer should be able to place some of these developments in the context of what had gone on in Germany before 1920, since cultural experimentation did not suddenly begin after the War. However, what were the conditions which allowed for such effervescence afterwards? Some awareness of European cultural developments generally would be helpful.

11 Assess the importance of developments in any *two* of the following in the Weimar Republic: literature; cinema; art; architecture; music.

This is a straightforward question provided you have studied any of these subjects in reasonable detail. A good answer should both describe the developments and place them in some overall context. Were the developments confined to a small group? Did they influence developments elsewhere?

12 Explain the connection between the coming to power of Hitler and the economic difficulties of the Weimar Republic.

The economic difficulties should be identified and analysed, throughout the years 1919-33. The various landmarks in the rise of Hitler and the Nazis also should be identified. Then the two phenomena should be related; for example, was it principally people suffering economically who voted for Hitler? Clearly there were connections, but was Hitler's rise to power also due to nationalist sentiment, anti-Communism and other factors?

13 'Economic collapse, outraged nationalism, anti-Marxism.' Which of these factors most aided the rise of the Nazis in Germany?

The three elements must be explained. Economic difficulties were serious from 1918, but catastrophic from 1929. 'Outraged nationalism refers principally to resentment over the Peace Treaty. How important was the sense of outrage amongst the population? How significant was anti-Marxism in winning support for the Nazis? The conclusion is likely to be that all three factors were important to a greater or lesser extent, perhaps at different times. You should attempt some synthesis of the causes, however much your answer is tentative and hedged around with qualifications.

14 To what extent does the weakness of the Weimar Republic explain Hitler's rise to power?

There are two principal strands to this question. Firstly there should be an analysis of the weakness of the Republic: this may be approached in terms of structural weaknesses (for example the Constitution), and policies or circumstances such as the 1923 Crisis. Secondly, you should analyse the rise of Hitler. Then relate the two. Was the rise of Hitler caused by the first factor; or was it partly coincidental? To what extent did Hitler simply exploit the weaknesses of the Republic and other circumstances better than its other enemies? Did the Republic have too few supporters? Was the Republic doomed anyway?

15 Why did the Weimar Republic fall to the Nazis rather than the Communists?

See specimen answer on page 101.

16 'A state within the state.' Is this a valid description of the German Army between 1890 and 1933?

Several points need to be developed: the constitution, size and leadership of the Army; its relationship with Parliament; the power and influence of its leaders; and the Prussian military tradition. The supremacy of the General Staff during the First World War must be explained and assessed. The impact of the Treaty of Versailles on the Army is important, as is the whole uneasy relationship of the Army with the Weimar Republic, symbolised in the relationship between Seeckt and Stresemann. The Army came close to participation in a coup. The fact that the Army did not intervene against the State does not disguise the fact that many Army officers barely tolerated the Republic. The Army was smaller after 1918, but still important, and it was to be Hitler who destroyed the influence of the Prussian military tradition much later.

17 How consistent were German imperialist and foreign policy aims between 1890 and 1933?

The issue of continuity is important here. You will have to analyse German imperial policy before the First World War, the formation of particular territorial aims during the War, who formulated them, and the degree to which these aims persisted in official and unofficial circles after 1918. What exactly were the aims? You should distinguish between overseas colonies and designs on Central and Eastern Europe. It is unlikely that you can answer this question without reference to the Fischer thesis and the whole debate about development and continuity in German history.

18 To what extent does the experience of Germany between 1890 and 1933 demonstrate the importance of the idea of continuity in history?

This is a difficult question requiring a carefully organised answer. What is meant by continuity? You should attempt to unravel various strands of history: political, economic and social – and then break them down still further into, for example, ideas and concepts such as militarism and nationalism. You cannot be expected to deal with all these in depth, but you should be able to analyse some of these factors, preferably with appropriate historiographical references.

19 Assess the contribution of any one historian to your understanding of German history during the period 1890-1933.

This question is an opportunity to discuss the work of any number of German or other historians who have written on this period, for example Fischer and his work on German imperialism and war aims. Do attempt an overall assessment and do not just describe the author's work.

20 Are personalities or issues more important in a study of German history between 1890 and 1933?

This is a wide-ranging question. You cannot be expected to deal with all aspects of the question, and there are no clear-cut answers, but you have considerable scope for discussion. The role of personalities – for example the Kaiser, Stresemann or Hitler – is reasonably straightforward. Issues could include problems of economic development, war guilt, nationalism, why the Right gained strength during the Weimar Republic – to name but a few. Choose carefully those issues you intend to write about, and cover as broad a span of the period as possible. You may find it helpful to consider how some historians have approached their subject.

Specimen Essay Answer

(See page 100)

Why did the Weimar Republic fall to the Nazis rather than the Communists?

Karl Erdmann declared that 'Weimar democracy was not destroyed by its adversaries, but by itself.' This is not a view that would be accepted by many historians. Certainly both the Nazi Party and the KPD, the German German Communist Party, new creations in the Weimar Republic, were fundamentally opposed to that institution. Between 1919 and 1933 there were occasions when many Germans expected, either in fear or hopeful anticipation, the demise of the Republic. Eventually the Nazis sounded its death-knell, beginning with the appointment of Hitler as Chancellor in January 1933. Hitler's success was to consign the KPD to official oblivion and a precarious underground existence in the Third Reich. The Weimar Republic experienced problems from its beginning, arising from its political structure, the problems it inherited and the policies it pursued. It is not the place here to discuss the issue of whether the Republic ever had a real chance of survival, given these problems. Rather the intention is to explain why it was the Nazis rather than the Communists who were in at the kill.

It should not be assumed that the rise of the Nazis to power was inevitable. Indeed, the beginnings of the movement in the aftermath of war were hardly auspicious. The Nazis were only one of several small Right-wing movements springing up. The growth of the Nazis was actually checked by the failed Putsch of 1923, and Hitler had to rebuild the Party afterwards. He then made the important decision to participate in the democratic political process and destroy the hated Republic from within.

Why did the Nazi Party grow in size and electoral support? The role of Hitler was obviously important as a charismatic orator and skilful propagandist. The movement, organised on para-military lines, had advantages over older, more conventional parties by virtue of its willingness to adapt its tactics and message in the struggle for power. The original Nazi Programme was designed to appeal to anti-Jewish, Socialist and nationalist tendencies in Germany. However, Hitler was prepared to adapt his appeal to a particular constituency – whether, for example, it was small farmers afraid of debt and ruin or businessmen afraid of the rise of Communism. The rise of the Nazi Party also had a distinctive regional pattern: it did not do particularly well in areas dominated by a Catholic or working-class Socialist ethos, although it appealed to some Catholics and workers. The Nazi share of the vote in national elections rose from 2.6 per cent in May 1928 to 18.3 per cent in September 1930 and 37.3 per cent in July 1932. It is common to attribute this advance to the decline of the parties and the influx into the Nazi Party of former non-voters, usually middle class. The Nazis certainly did well in rural areas and small towns where middle class values were strong. They performed less well among blue-collar workers, although some of the latter, particularly if they were unemployed after 1929, came over to the Nazis. Yet the Nazis also got votes in more affluent areas, and recent research suggests that the NSDAP was politically more mixed than other parties. In this sense it was the first German 'catch-all party of protest.'

What of the Communists? The KPD took part in elections from 1920, although like the Nazis it was anti-parliamentary in principle. The KPD represented only a small part of the German workers' movement and was widely distrusted. The internationalism of the Communists, in practice subordinate to the dictates of Moscow, contrasted with the German nationalism of the Right. The KPD suffered internal power struggles in the early 1920s and failed to exploit effectively crises like the 1923 inflation. In 1925 the KPD came under the leadership of Thälmann, subservient to Stalin. The fundamental weakness of the Communists was that they have engendered suspicion for their ill-organised attempts to seize power in the early years of the Republic; and at a time, from 1925, when they were a more coherent organisation, they were seen as subject to outside influence, and they failed to win the support of the majority of workers. Thälmann was no Hitler; and the KPD always operated from a narrower base of support than the Nazis. Also important was the gross tactical blunder of the KPD in concentrating its attacks on the more moderate SPD ('Social Fascists'), which simply helped open the way for Right-wing parties like the Nazis, who found the Communists a convenient scapegoat (along with the Jews) for Germany's ills, and a useful 'red bogey' with which to frighten the electorate in Hitler's direction.

The KPD did steadily increase its membership and electoral support as economic conditions worsened. From 1930 it attracted defectors from the SPD. By 1932 85 per cent of the KPD's membership came from the unemployed. The employed workers tended to stick with the moderate Socialist parties. In the words of one historian, the KPD was 'not so much the party of the revolutionary workers as the political representatives of the uprooted and dispossessed.' The KPD assumed that the crisis of world capitalism in the early 1930s would inevitably lead to their victory, but the leadership was more concerned to follow Stalin's dictates than to encourage a genuine radical mass working-class movement which might exhibit independent thought and action. One might go so far as to say that the leadership of both the KPD and SPD were more prepared to see the destruction of the German labour movement than swallow their differences and combine against the threat from the Right.

Nevertheless, in 1932 the KPD could still attract six million voters. Why then did the Weimar Republic fall with relative ease to the Nazis? The prospects for the survival of democracy were extraordinarily bleak after 1930. The Republic faced the crisis of the Great Depression, which magnified the impact of a fragmented party system and lack of a democratic consensus. Brüning's Government could not solve the political or economic crisis between 1930 and 1932. The succeeding Governments of von Papen and von Schleicher lacked support in Parliament or indeed on the streets. It was the Conservative Establishment which courted Hitler, hoping to use his mass support for their own ends. The Establishment could not tolerate the Red threat, whereas Hitler, for all his upstart vulgarity and the bully-boy tactics of his SA, was seen as a German patriot whose heart was basically in the right place. Therefore political manouvering replaced the democratic process, until Hitler was foisted on to Hindenburg as the saviour of Germany. Both the Nazis and the Communists were mass parties, but only one was acceptable to the political mandarins of the day. Blinded by their fear of the Left, the Conservatives underestimated Hitler's determination and independent will, and put him into power. The KPD contributed to this drama by their own tactical errors, but were perhaps in a near-impossible position: the Communists had probably reached the peak of their support, given their narrow social base; and yet they were reluctant to take the logical step of fomenting revolution against the system they despised – and probably they would have failed anyway had they attempted direct action.

By 1933 it was likely that if the Weimar Republic were to collapse, it would be to the Right rather than to the Left. In Hitler's first speech as Chancellor he claimed, 'Fourteen years of Marxism have undermined Germany. One year of Bolshevism would destroy Germany.' This was unconscious irony, since the German Communists had been so inept, and had had so many cards stacked against them, that their influence in the Weimar Republic had in the end been negligible other than as a bogey used by opponents for their own political ends. The Nazis were keen to claim that they had saved Germany from the Communist threat; but then Hitler and Goebbels were always masters of the Big Lie.

BIBLIOGRAPHY

There are extensive bibliographies on German history in specialist books. However, there are few easily accessible good books specifically on the period 1890-1914; there are many more on the First World War itself and the Weimar Republic. The few titles which follow should be useful to teachers and students, and are mostly available in paperback.

F. L. Carsten: *The Reichswehr And Politics 1918 To 1933* (Oxford University Press 1966). This book deals with the important role of the Army in the Republic.

E. Eyck: *History Of The Weimar Republic* – 2 Volumes (J. Wiley 1967). This study is detailed if somewhat dated.

J. W. Hiden: *The Weimar Republic* (Longman Seminar Studies 1974). This book contains relatively few documentary sources, but has a long introduction which discusses many of the issues from the 1918-1933 period.

H. Koch (Ed.): *The Origins Of The First World War: Great Power Rivalry And German War Aims* (2nd ed. London 1984). The Fischer thesis is discussed in this study, along with other issues.

E. Kolb: *The Weimar Republic* (Unwin Hyman 1988). This book is not easy, but is one of the few which treats the Weimar Republic as a subject worth study in its own right. It contains not just narrative, but surveys recent research, and includes a very detailed bibliography.

W. Laqueur: *Weimar: A Cultural History 1918-33* (Weidenfeld and Nicolson 1974). A detailed history of culture and the Weimar period generally.

A. J. Nicholls: *Weimar And The Rise Of Hitler* (Macmillan 1986). A useful general account.

D. O. Orlow: *A History Of The Nazi Party 1919-1933* (David and Charles 1971).

I. Porter and I. Armour: *Imperial Germany 1890-1918* (Longman Seminar Studies 1991). This book contains several documentary sources, but is most useful for a comprehensive survey of issues important in Imperial Germany.,

H. Wehler: *The German Empire 1871-1918* (Leamington Spa 1985). A useful study covering the period of Imperial Germany.

ACKNOWLEGEMENTS

The publishers wish to thank the following for their permission to reproduce material in this volume:

Barrie & Jenkins for the extract from *The Kaiser and his Times*, M. Balfour; Hamihs Hamilton for the extract from *The Origins of The Second World War*, A. J. P. Taylor (1961), copyright © A. J. P. Taylor, 1961, 1963; Longman Group UK for the extracts from *Bismark to Hitler*, J. C. G. Röhl (1970); Routledge for the extract from *The Weimar Republic*, E Kolb.

Every effort has been made to trace and acknowledge ownership of copyright. The publishers will be glad to make suitable arrangements with any copyright holders whom it has not been possible to contact.

The publishers would also like to thank the following for permission to reproduce copyright illustrations in this volume:

The National Gallery, Berlin/© DACS 1992 cover; p.63. Archiv Gerstenberg p.16; p.83. Snark International/Edimedia p.28. Archiv fur Kunst und Geschichte, Berlin/© DAC 1992 p.64 lower; p.86 lower. Estate of George Grosz/© DACs 1992 p. 42 both. Bayerisches Staatsbibliothek, Munich p. 56. Communist Party Library p.84. Otto Griebel/Deutshces Historisches Museum p.64 top. Ludwig Museum/Museen der Stadt Köln p.65. Bauhaus Archiv, Museum für Gestaltung, Berlin p.66 both. Paul Weber Estate/Wiener Library p.87. Wiener Library p.79; p.85. Akron Art Museum and Institute/© DACS 1992 p.86 top. Deutsches Staatsbibliothek Stifting Preussicher Kulturebesitz p.82.

INDEX